THE ART *of* CLOTHING CARE

THE ART *of* CLOTHING CARE

A GUIDE TO MAKING YOUR WARDROBE LAST

STEAMERY

Contents

Foreword

By Frej Lewenhaupt
Co-founder and CEO at Steamery

In Sweden, all middle school students have the opportunity to try both woodwork and sewing for one semester each before choosing which they'd prefer to continue with. This is the first time they get to make an individual decision about their education. For me, this choice was a given. After trying sewing for one semester, I knew I was going to dig deep into this subject.

Since then, I have been passionate about the clothing industry, both as a hobby and a profession. As a teenager, I earned pocket money by selling handmade crocheted beanies and upcycled clothes. I have worked in clothing stores and at a fashion agency in Australia. I studied to become a textile engineer at the Swedish School of Textiles in Borås and I worked at a clothing manufacturing company in Shanghai with some of the world's largest fashion brands.

Over this time I not only learned how to make clothes and where to source them from, but also the importance of taking care of the garments we buy. These days consumers buy clothes they love, but most don't have the proper tools or knowledge to make them last. I believe in changing this behavior and that's how Steamery was born.

Everything started in Shanghai in 2014 when I met my future co-founders Martin Lingner and Petra Ringström. Martin was a former management consultant and Petra was a silk fashion designer who frequently recommended her clients use steamers to care for the dresses she sold. We were all amazed by the steamer's ability to refresh textiles (without washing needed). At the time, there were no good-looking and modern clothing care products available on the market and we saw an opportunity to fill that void. Together the three of us launched Steamery as the first clothing care lifestyle brand with a mission to make it easier for people to keep their favorite clothes in excellent condition. Unsurprisingly, the steamer was the first product in our portfolio.

Ten years later, we offer a whole range of modern clothing care products that we believe will forever change the way we treat our clothes. Steamery was born out of an ambition to encourage people to be mindful of their relationship with the garments they buy. By creating innovative products designed for fast-paced urban lives, we hope to inspire a slow fashion lifestyle.

We are committed to helping you preserve the quality of your favorite clothes by reinventing the clothing care routine. With the proper care, your clothing can remain the best version of itself for as long as possible. We welcome you to Steamery and invite you to learn more about our philosophy of clothing care.

Introduction

At Steamery, we love caring for clothes – it's what we do. We care to bring out the colors and textures of textiles to make clothes fall in the way they were designed. We care for the comfort, quality and fit of our clothes. We care because our lives, experiences and memories are all intertwined with the clothes we love. We care because we want to give clothes a long life so they can be passed on to the next generation. We care because we want to reduce our environmental footprint and believe that our precious clothes should last forever.

The philosophy of clothing care is nothing new. Two generations ago, most people knew how to take care of their clothes, but since then these traditions have been forgotten and many garments are treated in the wrong way or thrown away too early.

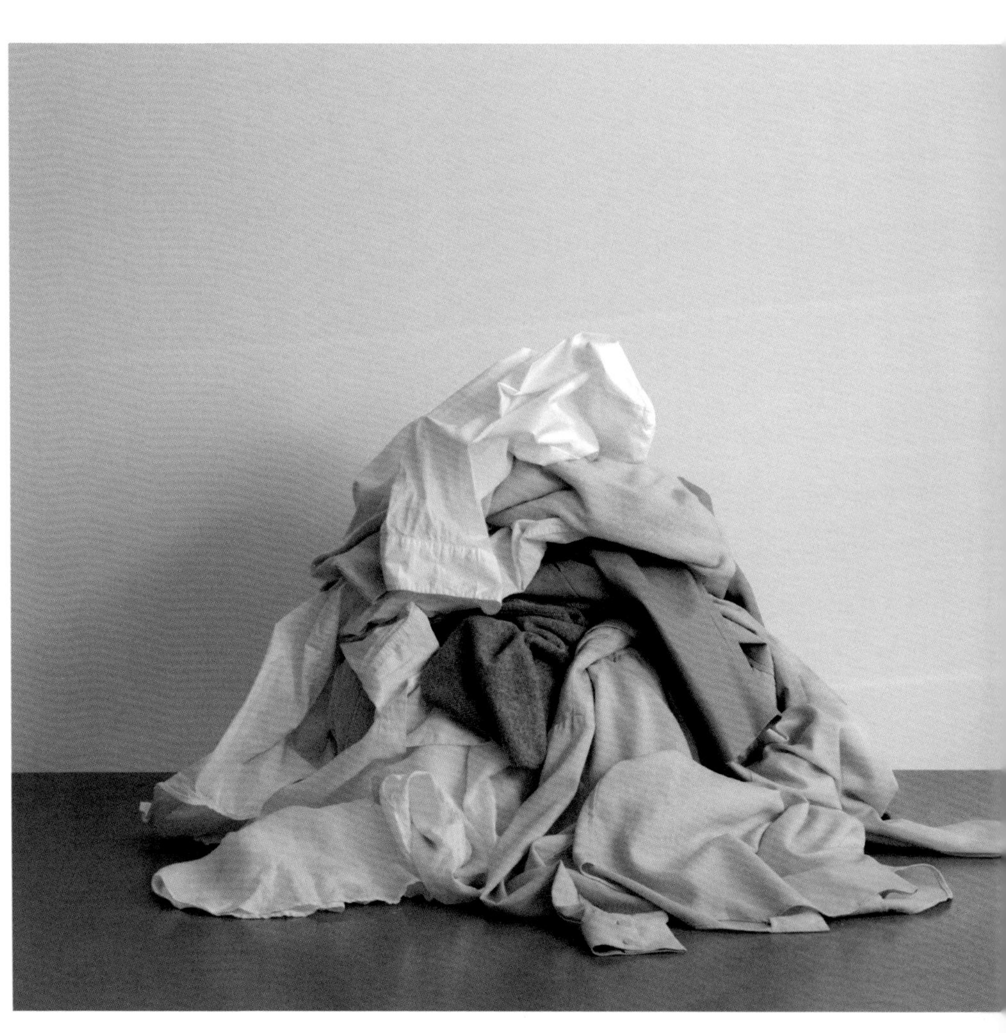

We have written this book to bring back the lost skill of clothing care, to teach others about the tools and techniques we can use to extend the life of our clothes. By shifting our mindset and viewing our clothes as lifelong companions and cherished items that can be passed down from generation to generation, we aim to make clothing care a simple and satisfying routine in our everyday life. And by doing this we can prevent massive amounts of textile waste and slow down the climate-damaging processes that are involved in the production of new clothes.

Making small changes

It has been estimated that Europeans only wear a piece of clothing seven to eight times, on average, before throwing it away. And, because of fast fashion, we buy 60 percent more clothes now than we did in 2000. Our modern way of living is so fast paced it can often feel overwhelming being bombarded with new fashion trends that make the clothes we already own look old and boring.

But what would happen if we started to turn our back on fast fashion trends and took a little extra time to slow down, to take pride in caring for our clothes and making them last as long as possible?

If we all made a few small changes, we could make a significant impact on the life cycle of our clothes. In the US, it's estimated that 85 percent of all textiles bought end up in landfills every year, where some materials take centuries to decompose. By buying less and finding joy in caring for the textiles already in our wardrobe, we can help to reduce the number of garments that go to waste each year.

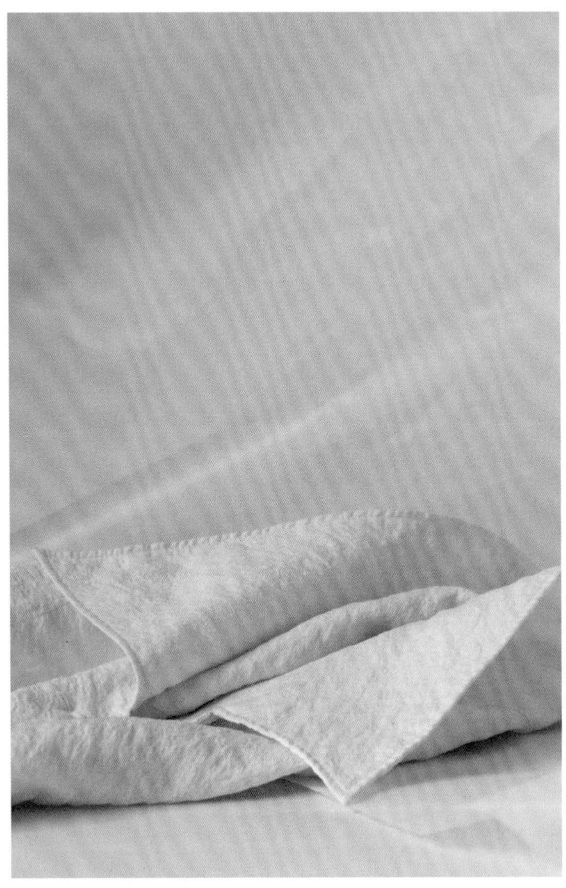

'Buy less. Choose well. Make it last.'

– Vivienne Westwood

Remember that you don't need to immediately overhaul your entire clothing care routine - instead you can use this book as inspiration to start making a few small changes to the way you view and treat your clothes.

BUY LESS: Start to think about what you love most about your current wardrobe. Take steps to slow down and assess whether you really need to buy garments as often as you do.

CHOOSE WELL: When shopping for clothes, it's better to invest in fewer quality garments that not only fit you, but suit your personality.

MAKE IT LAST: Learn how to take care of the clothes you already own to make them last for generations. Read the care label and learn about what you can do to take the best care of specific materials. The act of caring for our clothes can be a wonderfully meditative antidote to our hectic lives. Plus, if clothes are cared for properly, they often become even more beautiful over time as they develop their own unique patina.

CHAPTER 1

CURATING A CONSCIOUS WARDROBE

Fashion is such an important part of how we express ourselves - our clothes make a statement about who we are and how we want other people to perceive us. When we find clothes that look good, fit well and reflect our personality, it makes us feel great. But in modern life there's so much pressure to constantly update our wardrobes to keep up with the latest trends.

At Steamery, we believe there are easy steps we can take to move away from fast fashion and instead invest in clothes that will last. Today, it's often the case that consumers buy clothes they love, but do not know how to take care of them properly.

While shopping less can help to reduce your individual carbon footprint, it's only a small part of the story. As consumers, we have a responsibility to take care of the garments we already own. If we do this, our favorite clothes are more likely to last longer. So, when you find yourself in a clothing store, it helps to have basic knowledge of textiles to get a better idea of what garments you should be investing in.

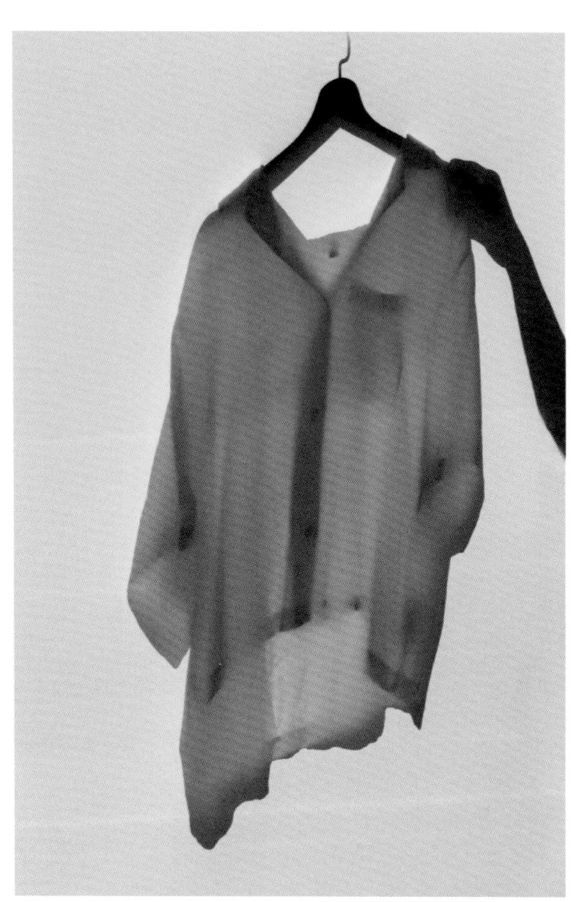

Shopping more consciously

When you need to add a garment to your wardrobe, it's important to be a conscious consumer - someone who only shops for what they need and who has the knowledge of how to care for their clothes to keep them looking great. It's a good idea to plan ahead before you hit the shops. Make a start by pinpointing the purpose of the garments that you really need. When and where will they be worn? What kind of fit and material would be suitable? And why not check if your local vintage shop carries anything similar before going to a store with only newly produced garments?

When deciding if you need to purchase a garment, there are a few simple questions you can ask yourself. Here are four questions we recommend, but you can always add your own personal considerations to this list. Why not have this checklist on your phone to look at when shopping?

1. CAN YOU WEAR IT 30 TIMES?

The #30wears challenge is as a great way to start shopping more consciously. Ask yourself if you would wear a piece of clothing at least 30 times. If the answer is yes, it's a good sign you could buy it and them aim to wear it for many more. 100 times would be a great goal.

2. THE SHOPPING LIST

Make a note of the gaps in your closet, and only buy clothes that fill those gaps. If you want to buy a piece of clothing but it is not on your shopping list, then you shouldn't go for it.

3. ASK SOME HARD QUESTIONS

Ask yourself some hard questions such as: 'If they didn't have it in my size, would I feel devastated?' Or: 'Am I ready to take on the responsibility of wearing and caring for this item until it's worn out or given to another person to use?' Your answers will help you decide if you need it or not.

4. SLEEP ON IT

Last, but not least, sleeping on it before you buy a piece of clothing is a great way to avoid an impulse purchase. Take a day to think about how the piece fits into your existing wardrobe and when you might use the garment. It's easy to get carried away and buy things you don't really need.

Building a capsule wardrobe you love

Cultivating a conscious wardrobe requires thinking and planning. One way to apply this to your everyday life in a practical way is to create a capsule wardrobe. The capsule wardrobe has become an antidote to seasonally trendy fast fashion garments. It is essentially a collection of garments that can be easily mixed and matched to create many different outfits. These are often versatile pieces in neutral colors with classic designs and silhouettes that complement each other.

Some prominent fashion brands have built a business model around the capsule wardrobe concept. Although they sell new clothes, they aim to design timeless garments that will look great for years, rather than announcing new clothing lines each season.

As well as the benefits of embracing slow fashion, a capsule wardrobe can also be a helpful remedy for decision fatigue. If you can never choose what to wear, having a wardrobe full of well-planned outfits should make it easier to put outfits together. After all, you can never really go wrong with a white button-up and a pair of black pants.

Building a well-curated wardrobe should not hinder your creativity or mute your personal style. It is simply a way to be more conscious about the long-term life of your wardrobe rather than shopping based on impulse or the latest trends. Play with colors and patterns and combine materials to create contrasts while making sure you buy clothes with intention. Here are a few tips to get you started:

1. ASSESS CURRENT WARDROBE

Take a good look at what you already own and identify your favorite pieces you can't go without. Think about why you love those garment, what emotions they evoke and how they make you feel when you wear them. In an ideal world, each piece in your wardrobe should make you feel this way. Then, take a look at what staple pieces make up your current closet. Perhaps you own a pair of high-waisted jeans, a white T-shirt or a trench coat with a classic silhouette? Pull out anything that you no longer wear or that does not fit you properly and consider if you want to alter, repurpose or donate these garments.

2. EXPLORE YOUR STYLE

Your capsule wardrobe should reflect your own unique style, so it's important to take some time to think about what that is. Think about which colors, patterns and textures make you feel confident and comfortable. If you're not sure what your personal style is, why not ask a trusted friend or family member for their own ideas – it will likely make for an insightful conversation!

3. CHOOSE A COLOR PALETTE

Deciding on a color palette is a great way to ensure the items in your capsule wardrobe will be easy to mix and match. Start with a basic color scheme and add a few accents that add more depth. You can also add some neutral colors like white, gray, black, navy or beige for versatile options. Choose colors that you love and look good on you. If you want to take it to the next level, you may consider doing a color analysis to determine which tones complement your natural features. There are plenty of resources for this online as well as professional stylists who offer personalized color analyses.

4. SELECT WARDROBE ESSENTIALS

Once you have a sense of your personal style and color palette, you can begin selecting the items that will make up your capsule wardrobe. These should include a mix of easy pieces that can be dressed up or down, such as a black suit, a classic white button-up and a pair of jeans. The goal is to have a small, yet versatile wardrobe, where a few items can create many different outfits. If possible, opt for high-quality items that will last a long time. You may need to spend a bit more on these pieces, but the benefit is that you will hopefully keep them for years to come.

5. ADD A FEW STATEMENT PIECES

It's also a good idea to include a few statement items to your capsule wardrobe to add some interest to your outfits. These could be bold jewelry pieces, a bright handbag or a top with a colorful print to pull out and wear on special occasions when you want to opt for a different look.

6. CARE FOR YOUR CLOTHES?

When you're choosing your capsule wardrobe, it's important to think about whether you can properly care for the garments you're picking. Your clothes will require different care routines depending on the material and, ideally, your clothes should last for a long time.

Capsule wardrobes are well worth the time and effort. By curating a collection of essential items that you love over time, you will be able to mix and match to create a variety of outfits with minimal effort. But the most important thing is to invest in clothes that you will love and appreciate for a long time. Stay true to your style and try not to fall for the latest trends. Instead, wear the clothes that you feel comfortable in and make your wardrobe a life-long companion.

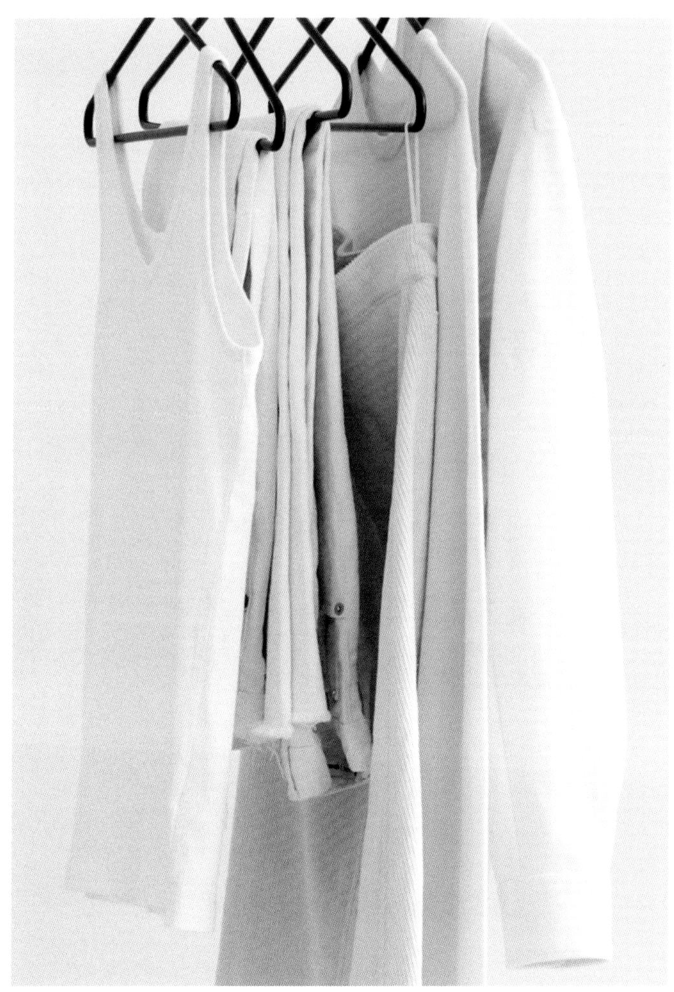

Quick quality checklist

When you're buying clothes, it's a good idea to spend a couple of minutes checking the quality of the garment. Our four suggestions are quick, easy and will hopefully help you to buy an item you'll be able to love and appreciate for years to come. Why not keep a note of this simple checklist on your phone to use on the go?

1. CHECK THE FABRIC

Feel the fabric in your hand. Is it comfortable, rich and durable? Or does it only look good on the hanger? It's also useful to study the care label. Are there high percentages of synthetic fibers, such as polyester or nylon? If the garment will be worn against your skin, would you prefer a more comfortable fabric such as cotton or silk? If there are more than four fibers in a blend, or if you can't see any specific percentages of the fiber content, then it might not be the best quality garment. There are some fabrics that can only be dry cleaned or hand washed - think about whether the suggested care routine is too complicated for you.

2. CHECK THE STITCHING

The stitching on a garment should be even, straight and secure. The stitches should not be too far apart and it's always a good idea to check for loose threads. Poorly constructed garments tend to have a minimal amount of thread holding everything together. You can test the strength of the stitching by gently pulling on the seams. For example, if a jersey item such as a T-shirt has an overlock seam (a stitch that sews over the edge of a piece of clothing), it's generally a better-quality garment if it also has a straight seam to secure it.

3. SEAM SLIPPAGES

Seam slippages might not be something you often check for on a garment, but they can cause holes in areas where the hem pulls the fabric, such as at the shoulders or under the arms. They're caused when the fabric frays on the seam, creating a gap which will eventually become a hole. They're also more common on glossier fabric such as silk or polyester. To check your garment, simply pull on the areas that will receive the most tension. If the seam opens, it is probably not a wise purchase.

4. CHECK THE DETAILS

Look at the buttons, zippers and other hardware on the garment to check if they are sturdy and functional. Try to avoid plastic details as they tend to break easily and can be sensitive to cold and heat. An easy check is to run the zipper up and down a few times to make sure it moves smoothly without too much resistance. You can also look on the back of the zipper to see if it's branded, as branded zippers are generally of better quality.

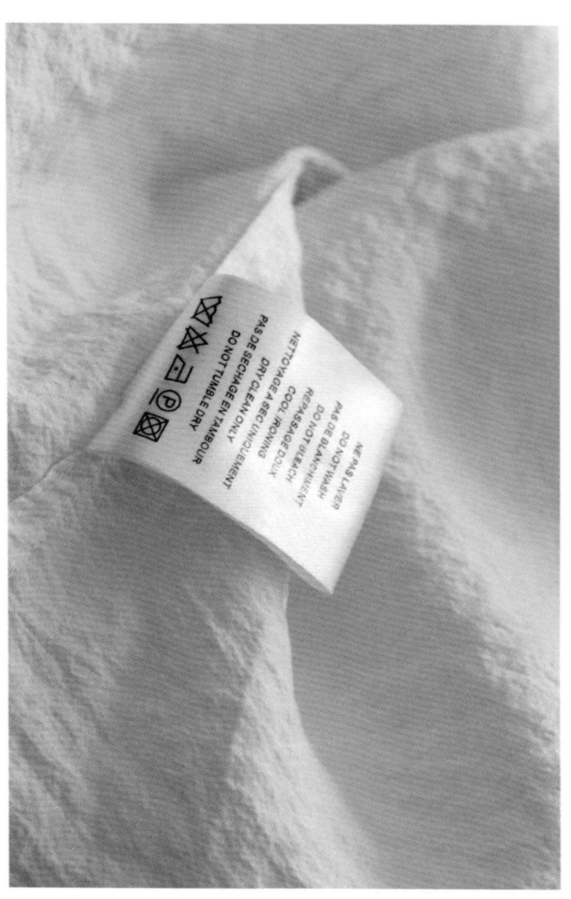
NE PAS LAVER
DO NOT WASH
PAS DE BLANCHIMENT
DO NOT BLEACH
REPASSAGE DOUX
COOL IRONING
NETTOYAGE A SEC UNIQUEMENT
DRY CLEAN ONLY
PAS DE SECHAGE EN TAMBOUR
DO NOT TUMBLE DRY

The care label

One of the first things you should look at on a piece of clothing is the garment's care label. The care label provides information on how to properly care for and clean the garment, one of the most important steps in creating a more conscious wardrobe.

As well as giving an insight into how to care for that specific clothing, it can give you some clues to the origin of the garment. However, textile production is a complex, labor-intensive industry and, from fiber to finished garment, there are many steps and many people involved in the production of one single piece of clothing. Here are some important things to look at when reviewing the care label:

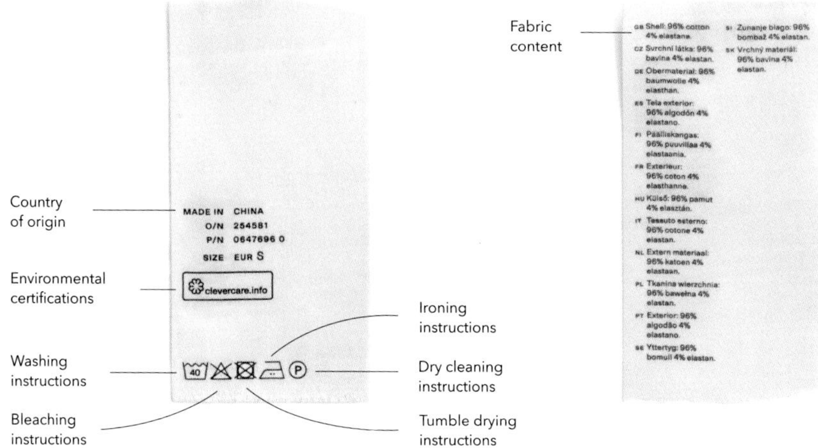

Country of origin
MADE IN CHINA
O/N 254581
P/N 0647696 0
SIZE EUR S
Environmental certifications
clevercare.info
Washing instructions
40
Bleaching instructions
Ironing instructions
Dry cleaning instructions
P
Tumble drying instructions
Fabric content
GB Shell: 96% cotton 4% elastane.
CZ Svrchní látka: 96% bavina 4% elastan.
DE Obermaterial: 96% baumwolle 4% elasthan.
ES Tela exterior: 96% algodón 4% elastano.
FI Pääliiskangas: 96% puuvillaa 4% elastaania.
FR Exterieur: 96% coton 4% elasthanne.
HU Külső: 96% pamut 4% elasztán.
IT Tessuto esterno: 96% cotone 4% elastan.
NL Extern materiaal: 96% katoen 4% elastaan.
PL Tkanina wierzchnia: 96% bawełna 4% elastan.
PT Exterior: 96% algodão 4% elastano.
SE Yttertyg: 96% bomull 4% elastan.
SI Zunanje blago: 96% bombaž 4% elastan.
SK Vrchný materiál: 96% bavina 4% elastan.

WASHING INSTRUCTIONS:
Always look at the washing instructions to see if you are prepared to take care of the garment in the way that is required. Are you buying a garment that needs to be dry cleaned or hand washed? The care label will often include specific instructions on how to wash the garment, such as the appropriate water temperature and whether it can be machine washed or tumble dried.

IRONING INSTRUCTIONS:
Also take a look at the ironing instructions. These will show whether the garment can be ironed and, if so, how hot the iron should be.

DRY CLEANING INSTRUCTIONS:
The care label can often indicate whether a garment can be dry cleaned or not and, if so, what type of dry-cleaning solvent is safe to use.

BLEACHING INSTRUCTIONS:
There may also be instructions on whether the garment can be bleached or not and, if so, what type of bleach is safe to use.

OTHER CARE INSTRUCTIONS:
Look for other specific care instructions, such as whether the garment should be hung or laid flat to dry and whether it should be washed inside out.

FABRIC CONTENT:
Care labels typically list the fabric content of the garment, which can help you understand how the garment will look and feel, as well as how it should be cared for. For example, a garment made from 100 percent cotton may be more prone to shrinkage than a garment made from a synthetic blend.

COUNTRY OF ORIGIN:
Care labels may also list the country where the garment was put together. This can be useful information for consumers who are interested in supporting locally made or ethically produced garments. However, the label won't tell you everything about where the garment was made. For example, you won't be able to tell where the fiber is produced or where the fabric was dyed. Unfortunately, it is also difficult to deduce anything about production conditions on the label, for example if the workers who sewed the garment receive a decent wage for their work or how they are treated.

MANUFACTURER INFORMATION:
Care labels may also list the name and contact information of the manufacturer, which can be useful for contacting the company if you have any questions or concerns about the garment.

HAZARD WARNINGS:
Care labels may also include hazard warnings, such as 'flammable' or 'contains small parts', which can be important safety information for consumers.

ENVIRONMENTAL CERTIFICATIONS:
It's also good to look for certificates. If the garment is cotton, it's a big plus if it follows the Global Organic Textile Standard (GOTS), is Fair Trade Certified, has Better Cotton Initiative (BCI) certification or is OEKO-TEX* Standard 100 certified. These are common certifications that go some way to ensuring the ethical production of the cotton your garment is made from. However, this is a complex issue and each certification has different goals and requirements.

Materials and what to look for

The clothes we wear are made from a wide variety of different fibers, each with their own unique properties, strengths and weaknesses. And, as a consumer, it's useful to have basic knowledge of these materials so you can make the right choices. Do you want a material that's cool and breathable, or are you after something water-resistant and elastic?

We believe that it's important to make conscious choices while shopping, so you can curate a wardrobe of materials that you love and can care for properly. Here, we explain the basics of plant, animal, semi-synthetic and synthetic fibers.

Plant fibers

Cotton, Linen, Hemp, Bamboo

Plant fibers are breathable and feel light and airy against the skin. They are comfortable to wear in hot weather, durable and generally easy to care for. Plant fibers are also biodegradable and, when cared for properly, can age beautifully over the years. Linen in particular is a more sustainable option, as it doesn't require as much water or chemical usage during production as other fibers. Cotton uses a lot of resources to produce but often lasts longer than linen, which makes it a favorable choice for second-hand clothing.

Plant fibers can also shrink in the wash, so they need to be cleaned with care. Linen and hemp can wrinkle easily, so it's best to steam them regularly to keep your clothes looking good.

Animal fibers

Wool, Silk, Cashmere, Mohair, Angora, Alpaca

Animal fibers are known to have excellent insulation properties. Wool, for example, is great at trapping heat, which will help you stay warm on a cold winter day. Others, such as silk and cashmere, are soft to the touch and feel comfortable against the skin. Wool and cashmere are naturally anti-bacterial and don't need to be washed frequently.

However, like plant fibers, animal fibers are prone to shrinkage, and should be washed with care. Delicate protein fibers such as wool and silk should also be washed using a laundry detergent that nourishes and protects natural fibers. Cashmere wool also naturally pills and will need extra care to maintain its condition and keep it looking great.

Semi-synthetic fibers

Viscose, Modal, Lyocell, Acetate, Cupro

Semi-synthetic fibers are man-made fibers made from wood pulp or cellulose that undergo a chemical process to become soft and pliable, such as viscose, rayon, modal and lyocell. They can be engineered to possess a wide range of properties such as enhanced strength, moisture-wicking or breathability. This versatility makes them suitable for various applications in the textile industry. Compared to synthetics, semi-synthetic fibers have excellent absorbency, allowing the fibers to wick moisture away from the body and keep the clothes dry. They also have a smooth texture.

The production of semi-synthetic fibers involves chemical treatments, such as dissolving natural materials in solvents and then regenerating them into fibers. While the manufacturing process of semi-synthetic fibers can also be very energy and water intensive, lyocell is an exception as chemicals are reused in the manufacturing process. And while semi-synthetic fibers are generally more environmentally friendly than fully synthetic fibers such as polyester, they may not be as biodegradable as natural fibers.

Synthetic fibers

Polyester, Nylon, Acrylic, Spandex

Synthetic fibers are formed by chemical means and are mainly derived from petroleum. Like semi-synthetic materials, they can be made to possess a wide range of properties, including elasticity and tensile strength. They also tend to be more durable which makes them a better choice for heavier duty items.

In general, acrylic should be avoided since it is a very fragile and heat-sensitive fiber that is often used as a diluting agent in material mixtures to keep costs down. Synthetic materials also form static electricity easily, which causes the fabrics to attract dust. They are not readily biodegradable and can remain in landfill for up to 200 years. Their production requires valuable non-renewable resources, mainly petroleum and natural gas. Toxic chemicals are also often used in the manufacturing process.

72% Polyester
27% Viscose
1% Elastane
EUR 36
UK 10
Made in Portugal
Wash with similar colours
Please wash with respect
of nature.

Fiber blends

When you look at a care label, it's very common to see more than one textile fiber in a blend. Often, you'll come across a shirt that is 80 percent cotton and 20 percent polyester, which means that the fabric is made from a blend of both natural and synthetic fibers. Blending different fibers in one garment means the material can be engineered to suit the customer's specific needs. For instance, socks that are reinforced with synthetic fibers in a blend will, in most cases, last longer than those made from 100 percent natural fibers.

Unfortunately, it's currently very difficult to recycle fiber blends, because they are made up of different materials. However, you can still upcycle or repurpose them in order to extend their lifespan.

Patina

Like us, materials age and develop over the years. And if a garment is loved and cared for properly, then it is likely to become more beautiful as it ages. The concept is, the more you wear them, the better. This is because, over time, materials develop patina - a rather amazing phenomenon that is perhaps better known in the realm of antiques. Patina is a thin layer that forms on the surface of certain materials over time due to natural weathering. As well as giving a garment a unique look, it can also protect the underlying material from further corrosion or deterioration.

Patina often increases the value of clothes, especially if the garment is made from a material that ages well. Clothes that have developed patina have a more unique, vintage look. Patina is influenced by factors such as the wearer's body shape, usage patterns and environmental conditions. This uniqueness adds value to the clothing as it becomes a one-of-a-kind piece that stands out from newer or similar items.

In some cases, the presence of patina can indicate that the garment is made from high-quality materials and was constructed with superior craftsmanship. The fact that it has stood the test of time, showing signs of wear without falling apart, can be seen as a testament to its durability and longevity. This perception of quality can positively impact the value of the clothing.

In the world of vintage or high-end fashion, the presence of patina can signify the authenticity of the garment, especially if it is a sought-after or rare piece. It adds a sense of history and uniqueness, making the item more desirable to collectors and enthusiasts. As clothes develop patina, they can often become more and more comfortable over time, a bit like the process of breaking in a pair of new shoes.

At Steamery, we believe that taking time to appreciate and learn more about patina can be an antidote to the idea that everything in your wardrobe should look 'new'. Instead, start to embrace the idea that it's much better to enjoy a unique piece with its own history and personal significance.

The process of patina begins as soon as you start to wear clothes. Its development can vary depending on a few factors, such as the quality of the material, how you use it and the level of care.

Textiles that develop patina

Any fiber or fabric can potentially develop patina over time, if it is exposed to regular wear and use. These are some of the textiles that are more commonly known to develop patina.

DENIM: Denim ages easily and develops patina when used and washed. The patina of denim can give the fabric a unique color and texture, making it more attractive. Different types of patina can form, depending on how it is used and washed. For example, frayed areas may form on the knees, seams and pockets, or there might be a general fading of the fabric's color.

LEATHER: Patina is common on leather and is often sought after for products such as bags, shoes, wallets and belts. The patina on leather can form naturally over time through normal use, from scratches and marks. It can also make the leather softer and more flexible, while protecting it from further wear and tear.

WOOL: Wool is a natural fiber that can develop patina over time with regular wear and exposure to the elements. As wool fibers become matted and worn, the material can take on a unique texture and appearance.

SILK: Silk can develop patina, especially if it is exposed to light and air. Over time, the silk fibers may become slightly discolored, giving the material a soft, subtle sheen.

LINEN: Linen garments, such as shirts, pants or dresses, can develop patina with regular wear and washing. The fabric may become softer, smoother and acquire a slightly worn-in look, giving it character.

CANVAS: Canvas is a sturdy fabric that can develop patina with regular use and exposure to the elements. The canvas will become worn and faded, taking on a unique charm.

Patination

While it's great to appreciate the beauty of patina and to source pre-loved clothes that have formed their own unique look and feel, clothing companies often apply a fake patina to newly made denim. Unfortunately, this process, called 'patination', damages the fabric before it is even worn once.

If you are buying new denim, we would recommend that you avoid products that appear aged. It is so much more worthwhile to invest in clothing that hasn't been damaged in the manufacturing process. Over time, you can help it develop its own natural patina.

Simple second-hand hacks

If you've always bought new clothes from big fashion brands, exploring the world of pre-loved garments can feel really daunting. But at Steamery, we think that shopping on the second-hand market is even more enjoyable, and rewarding, than buying new.

Shopping on the second-hand market unlocks the world's largest selection of clothing, including rare gems that have aged beautifully and increased in value over time. Delving into the unique items on offer is a great way to explore your personal style and express your individuality. It's also more of a sustainable choice as you're extending the life cycle of clothes that are already in circulation.

And if you have an item of clothing in your wardrobe that you've fallen out of love with, sell it to ensure it's going to be used by someone else, rather than sitting in landfill.

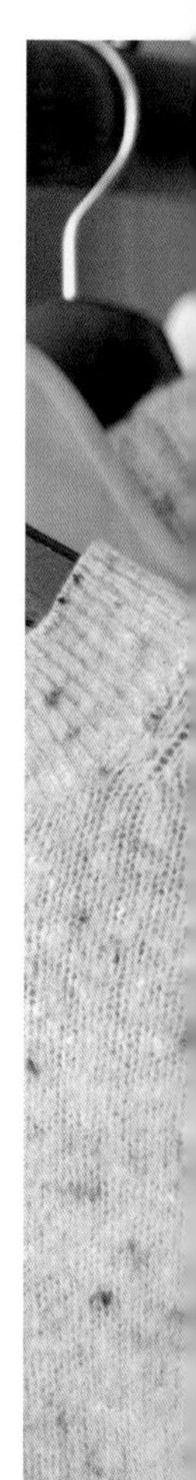

For first-time vintage shoppers, it takes a bit of time to figure out the way to buy pre-loved clothes that works best for you - you might prefer to look in charity shops, explore vintage boutiques or to buy from private sellers online. If you're completely new to it, take it slow and maybe challenge yourself to buy one pre-loved item when you would have otherwise bought new.

To help you on this journey, we have gathered some quick and easy tips to inspire your adventures in the second-hand clothing market.

Shopping and selling second-hand

Like with buying new clothes, there's a variety of different ways to shop second-hand. It all depends on who you are and why you are buying the garment. What sort of budget are you on? Are you looking to sell the garment and want to make money from it? What's the most sustainable choice? Is it an everyday garment or something you will use occasionally? Your answers affect where you should look for the garment. Here are our best tips:

APPS OR ONLINE STORES: Shop and sell second-hand from private sellers on apps or websites such as Facebook Marketplace, eBay, Sellpy, Vestiaire Collective, Vinted or Depop – it's likely you might find a great deal from a local seller. Some of these sites hold auctions where the highest bidder buys the garment, while others are more like regular online stores.

VINTAGE SHOPS: Shopping second-hand in vintage stores is a great way to get high-quality second-hand garments and a good mix of brands. The downside is that these clothes can be a little more expensive compared to clothes you buy online.

THRIFT AND CHARITY SHOPS: These stores are typically run by charities or non-profit organizations. Here the prices are usually cheaper than in other second-hand shops, but the quality can vary.

SOCIAL MEDIA AND NEIGHBORHOOD GROUPS: Searching for pre-loved items on social media is an easy and fast way to find and shop second-hand. You just have to find the right ones. Ask friends and family if they know of any local or bigger groups or search with keywords to find those that match your needs.

Sprucing up pre-loved clothes

A widespread myth about second-hand clothes is that they are dirty and unsanitary. This is not necessarily true. In fact, new clothes from the factory are often not clean when they are delivered. Plus, once you've bought second-hand clothes, there are lots of ways to make them feel like new again before you hang them in your wardrobe.

HANG OUTSIDE TO AIR FOR DAYS

Airing clothes is ideal for natural materials that can breathe, like wool or silk. Fresh air allows for the natural dissipation of odorous molecules that may have stuck in the fibers, leaving them smelling fresher. Even if the garment smells okay to begin with, it can still be a useful thing to do in order to fully refresh the textile fibers and recreate the feeling of a brand-new garment.

SOAK IN WHITE DISTILLED VINEGAR

Garments bought online that arrive smelling unpleasant can be saved if you give them a bath. Fill a bath or a basin with lukewarm water and add 100 ml of white distilled vinegar. Let the garment soak overnight and follow up by washing it in the washing machine.

WASH WITH A SUITABLE LAUNDRY DETERGENT

For synthetic or cotton items we recommend you wash them with a laundry detergent that has been specially developed for sweaty workout clothes and other odor-prone textiles.

SPRITZ WITH A FABRIC SPRAY

The quickest and easiest way to spruce up garments and disguise bad smells is by spritzing the garment with a scented fabric spray that neutralizes odors. However, don't try this on extremely delicate clothes, such as vintage silk, lace or other types of delicate fabrics that should not be exposed to water.

BED BUGS AND OTHER VERMIN

If you suspect that your vintage garments have attracted vermin, put them in the freezer (-18°C/-0.4°F) for at least three days. Once they've defrosted, wash the garments according to the instructions on the care labels. Bed bugs are also killed when garments are washed at a minimum of 60°C/140°F, but not all clothes can withstand those temperatures so it's best to be careful and put them in the freezer instead.

STEAM CLOTHES BACK INTO SHAPE

Clothes that have been washed before being sold might have lost their natural shape. This can happen to almost any type of garment that isn't cared for in the right way. To remedy this, steam through the whole garment thoroughly before judging whether the fit is bad or that the garment is just a little bit abused from the washing. Read more about unshrinking sweaters in Chapter 2.

Selling your clothes online

If you're getting rid of items in your wardrobe, selling your clothes on the second-hand market is a great way to contribute to a circular way of living. If you're thinking about selling there are a few things you need to know to prepare yourself, and your clothes:

SPARK INTEREST WITH THE RIGHT DESCRIPTION

Always write the specific brand and model name in your ad. Specify what material the garment is made of, especially if it is an exclusive textile such as wool or silk. Include styling tips to paint a livelier image for potential buyers and be sure to include sizes and measurements, especially for pants or jeans as cuts and designs can vary a lot.

Measurements to include:

- Pants and jeans: waist and inside leg length (measure across the waist and on the inside of the leg).
- Dresses: length and sleeve length (from top to bottom and from the armpit to the cuff).
- Skirts: waist and length.
- Jackets and coats: length from collar to hem, and sleeve length.
- Shoes: inside length and if they are considered narrow, normal or wide (you can often find this information at the manufacturers' websites).

DESCRIBE THE CONDITION IN DETAIL

When purchasing clothes on the second-hand market, everyone understands that the clothes are used. But for the sake of transparency, always mention if there are stains and where they are located - better yet, take a photo. Mention if there are any loose hems or threads. Also be sure to describe what is good about the garment - you don't want to scare people off.

Useful phrases to describe a garment's condition:

- 'NWT' (new with tags) - Unused garments with the label still attached can be described like this.
- 'New' - There is no evidence the garment has been worn at all.
- 'Good, used condition' - Vibrant colors, no loose threads or stains, but it has been used and washed.
- 'Used, but still has a lot to offer' - This is a positive way of describing a garment with defects or with evident traces of being worn.

It's also a good idea to include info about how you have taken care of the garment:

- Say if you have been using an unscented detergent and fabric softener or not (especially appreciated by people with sensitive noses or allergies).
- If you are a pet owner (appreciated by people with allergies).
- If the garment has been dry cleaned recently.
- Whether you are a smoker or not.

TAKE APPEALING PHOTOS

You will need various kinds of photos for your ad. Use your phone camera and shoot with the flash turned off, preferably in daylight. Place your garment in front of a neutral background - somewhere next to a window is a good start but be mindful of where you place the garment as you want to avoid hard shadows or backlight.

Helpful pictures to include in the ad:

- One full image of the garment.
- One product image that will display how it looks on.
- Pictures that show any defects.
- A picture of the care label (as a potential buyer, you may want to know how to take care of the garment).

ENSURE SMOOTH SHIPPING

Reuse old packages, such as brown paper bags or old shoe boxes, or specific mailing bags easily found online, and please consider using a courier that offers traceable shipping, as this is safer for you and the buyer.

SELLING YOUR CLOTHES OFFLINE

Vintage shops often operate by selling clothes on behalf of the original owner. The owner will receive a commission when the garment is sold. Normally the commission is 40-50 percent, but it's best to do your own research or ask your local vintage store. Some brands also have their own second-hand vintage markets, where they only sell second-hand items from their brand.

Second-hand items to avoid

At Steamery, we believe you should buy as many of your clothes as possible on the second-hand market. However, not everything is made to be worn by different people. While we wouldn't advise buying these items from an unknown seller, you could buy some of these items second-hand if you know and trust the seller.

UNDERWEAR: Obviously, due to hygiene reasons, it's not advisable to buy underwear or swimwear that has been worn by someone else. Second-hand socks are also likely to be worn out and won't last very long.

SAFETY HELMETS: Helmets, for a bike or motorcycle, shouldn't be bought used as they might not provide adequate protection if they have been involved in an accident.

BEDDING: Items such as mattresses, duvet covers and sheets can harbor allergens and bed bugs, which means they shouldn't be bought second-hand.

PERSONAL PROTECTIVE EQUIPMENT (PPE): Any type of PPE, such as hard hats, safety goggles or gloves, should not be bought second-hand as their effectiveness may have been compromised.

CAR SEATS FOR INFANTS: Car seats should be purchased new so they meet the current safety standards.

ultra boost

JOGGING SHOES: While new jogging shoes tend to be very expensive, it is likely that the previous owner will have worn the shoes out already. It's estimated that running shoes have a lifespan of 300 – 1000 km, so any sports shoes bought on the second-hand market are likely to have lost any cushioning support.

Recycling

Recycling is a good option for clothing that is beyond repair or too worn out to be sold. Recycling can help to reduce the environmental impact of discarded clothing. But today, only a fraction of the textiles that are collected are recycled. Due to a lack of large-scale solutions for sorting and recycling textiles, only 1 percent of used clothes actually get recycled into new ones. It is also important to bear in mind that a recycled garment only has a 5–10 percent lower climate impact than a garment made from virgin fibers, because all the other steps in production are carried out in exactly the same way.

Buying clothes from recycled materials can therefore falsely reassure us that we're being environmentally friendly and allows us to consume more. Despite this recycling is definitely a step in the right direction even if it's not perfect yet. The demand for good recycling is high and luckily there are many companies working to improve recycling for textiles. Read more about these initiatives in Chapter 4.

RENTING

In a perfect world, we would be able to rent or swap all the clothes we need for all occasions. Even if this is not the reality today, there are several options and start-ups for renting clothes on the market. These companies offer access rather than ownership. The only downside with renting fashion is that it can sometimes be quite expensive compared to buying second-hand.

SWAPPING CLOTHES

In 2008 one of the world's first swapping events started, Leeds Community Clothes Exchange in the UK. Since then, swapping communities and swapping events have become more and more popular within the slow fashion movement. The idea is to turn up with selected clothes from your wardrobe and exchange them with others for free. Swapping clothes is easy, accessible and fun. Today there are even companies offering swapping solutions for consumers. So, if your friends or colleagues are up for it, try to organize a clothing swap at home or at work. Clothes often carry sentimental value, so lending your garments can be a perfect solution if you don't feel ready to sell or swap.

DONATING TO THRIFT AND CHARITY SHOPS

Donating clothes to thrift shops has several advantages. Many shops partner with local charities or social programs, ensuring that the donated clothing reaches individuals and families who may not be able to buy new clothes. Donating is also great from a circular perspective. Instead of throwing away unwanted clothes, donating them allows them to be reused and repurposed.

With this said, it is important to remember that donating does not mean we should buy more. We must keep in mind that these stores receive a large amount of clothes every year and as little as 15–20 percent of these clothes actually get sold. The rest are sent to recycling companies, who resell clothing to developing countries, causing a waste problem over time. These clothes sometimes travel the world several times before ending up in markets or landfill sites.

Store and organize

Organizing and storing your beloved clothes in a smart way is crucial to make a curated and more conscious wardrobe. We have gathered some tips on how to organize and store your textiles gently and neatly.

How to organize your wardrobe

LET GO AND START FRESH

Start by discovering what is hiding in the back of your closet. Take out all your clothes and sort them into different categories. For example, put your sweaters in one pile, pants in another pile, and so on. Go through each category and ask yourself why you have saved these particular items. Consider how often they are used and how well they fit you.

COLOR COORDINATE

To feel inspired, organize your closet in a way that is easily accessible and easy on the eyes. One way to do this is to color coordinate all your garments and hang all your prints on one side. Alternatively, you can try to pre-plan outfits by hanging matching items together. Have fun with it and organize your clothes in a way that is functional and looks aesthetically pleasing to you.

OPTIMIZE YOUR CLOSET SPACE

This is also an excellent opportunity to rotate the garments and make room for the clothes that were previously hidden in the back of the closet. Let yourself fall in love with your old clothes again and discover new ways to combine, match and layer different items of clothing.

Updating your wardrobe without buying more

Do you have a closet full of clothes, yet feel like you have nothing to wear? Many of us have been there, but there are many ways to feel inspired by the clothes that already hang in your closet.

ROTATE REGULARLY

One of the easiest ways to refresh your closet is to regularly rotate your garments and display old favorites you may have forgotten that you own. This is especially helpful if you store your clothes in a chest of drawers where they are out of sight.

Just as you would put away holiday decorations, you can do the same with your seasonal clothes.

REPEAT YOUR FAVORITE OUTFITS

We've been conditioned to think that it's shameful to wear the same clothes too many times. People who parade a seamlessingly endless number of clothes online set an unrealistic standard for people to live up to.

In fact, from a slow fashion perspective, repeating outfits is the best thing you can do. We need to make do with what we already have. Keep wearing your favorite pieces with pride.

UPCYCLE

This is a fun and great way to find new inspiration in the clothes you already own. Upcycling means that you remake clothes you don´t use anymore into something new to increase their value or give their a new lease on life. Why not cut a piece of old denim jeans into a pair of shorts or make a bag out of your old T-shirt? Upcycling is not as hard as you might think it is. Read more about how to mend and upcycle textiles in chapter 3.

While buying clothes can make us feel good in the short term, it is so much more fulfilling to love and care for the clothes we already have. We encourage you to slow down, to take time to consider what items you really care about in your wardrobe and whether you need to add to your personal collection.

By taking a more mindful approach, we can take steps toward buying less and ensuring that the garments we do own are kept beautifully and will last.

As you think about your own wardrobe, we invite you to draw inspiration from what you already have at your fingertips. Start swapping and borrowing from your friends and family. When you need to buy something, think about visiting a second-hand store in your area. And when you would have otherwise thrown a garment away, consider giving it to a friend or selling it, so someone else can enjoy it just as much as you have.

By embracing slow fashion, we can take pride in what we have and truly value the artistry at work in our wardrobes.

CHAPTER 2

CLOTHING CARE, MADE EASY

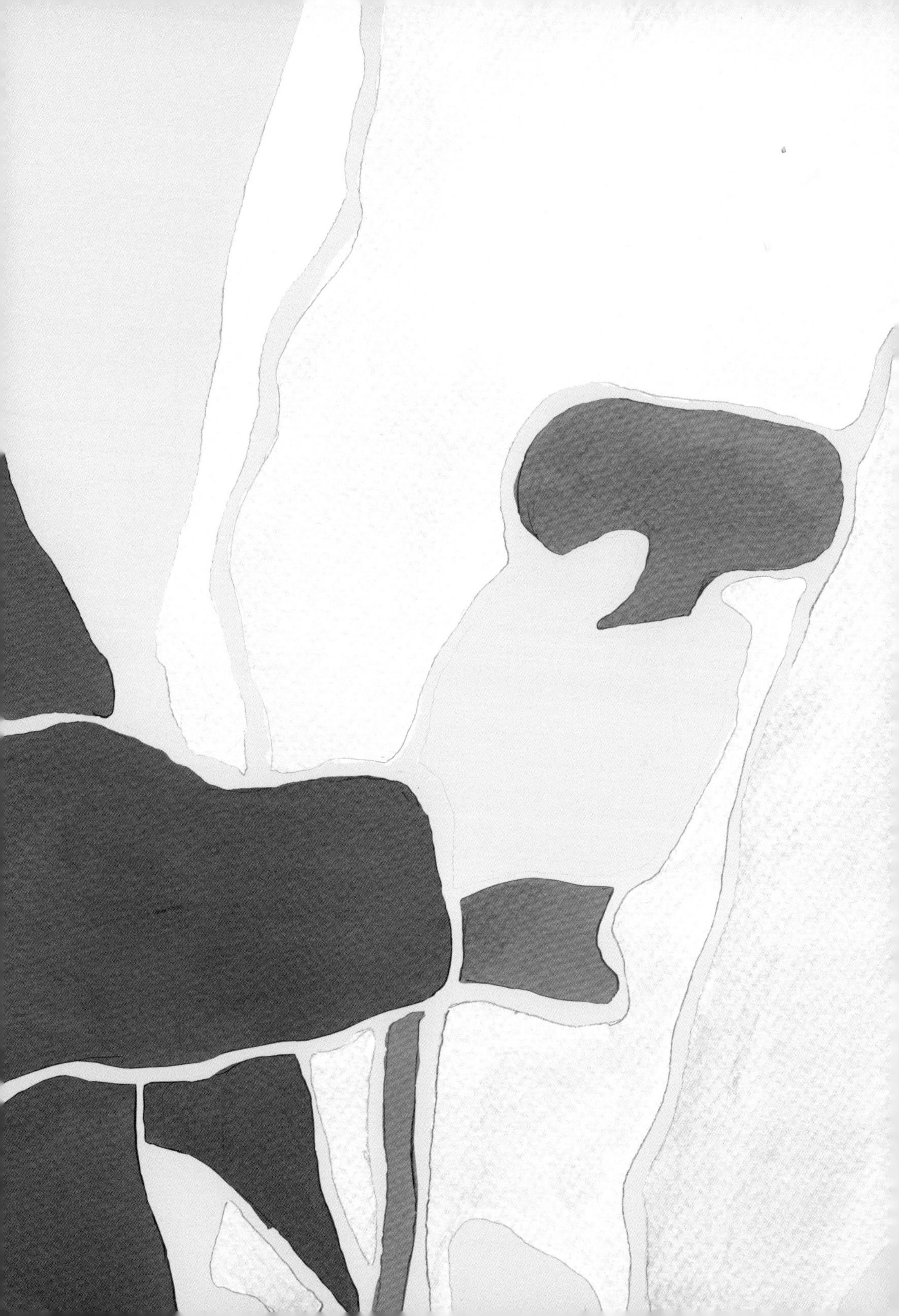

Two generations ago, most people knew how to care for their clothes – but in the years since, that knowledge has disappeared. We want to reintroduce people to the fulfillment that comes when you can care for your clothes properly.

To the uninitiated, it might initially seem that clothing care is difficult or boring. But once you have a basic understanding of how to look after your garments, you'll find that maintaining your wardrobe is quick, easy and might even save you time – it's all about making little changes to your routines.

Think about something else you value highly – it might be a car, a house, a watch or even your own health. What would happen if you didn't care for it? It's the same thing with the clothes you own. If you have the knowledge and the tools to care for them in the right way, then they will last longer. After all, the clothes in our wardrobes can be some of our most precious belongings. If you truly love the clothes you own, prolonging the life of your garments is one of the most rewarding things you can do.

Clothing care through the ages

The history of clothing care is deeply intertwined with the development of various techniques and technologies to maintain and preserve garments.

ANCIENT TIMES

Clothing care was focused on cleaning and removing dirt and stains. Items were washed in rivers and lakes, or with water and detergents made from plant extracts or animal fats.

MIDDLE AGES AND EARLY MODERN PERIOD

People began to explore different techniques to maintain their clothing, including using vinegar, lemon juice or natural bleaching agents to remove stains. Sometimes soap made from animal fats was used to wash clothes.

18TH AND 19TH CENTURIES

The development of mechanical washing machines, powered by water or hand-cranked mechanisms, made it easier to clean garments. People also started to use more sophisticated detergents and bleaching agents.

EARLY 20TH CENTURY

Mass production of electric washing machines, irons and steam irons revolutionized the process of laundering clothes. Dry cleaning became more prevalent, allowing for the cleaning of more delicate fabrics.

LATE 20TH CENTURY

Washing machines became more efficient and dryers were introduced. The rise of synthetic fabrics and blends presented new challenges in clothing care, as they often required specific washing and drying instructions to prevent damage.

PRESENT DAY

Clothing care continues to evolve with the advent of smart appliances and sustainable clothing care practices have gained a new popularity.

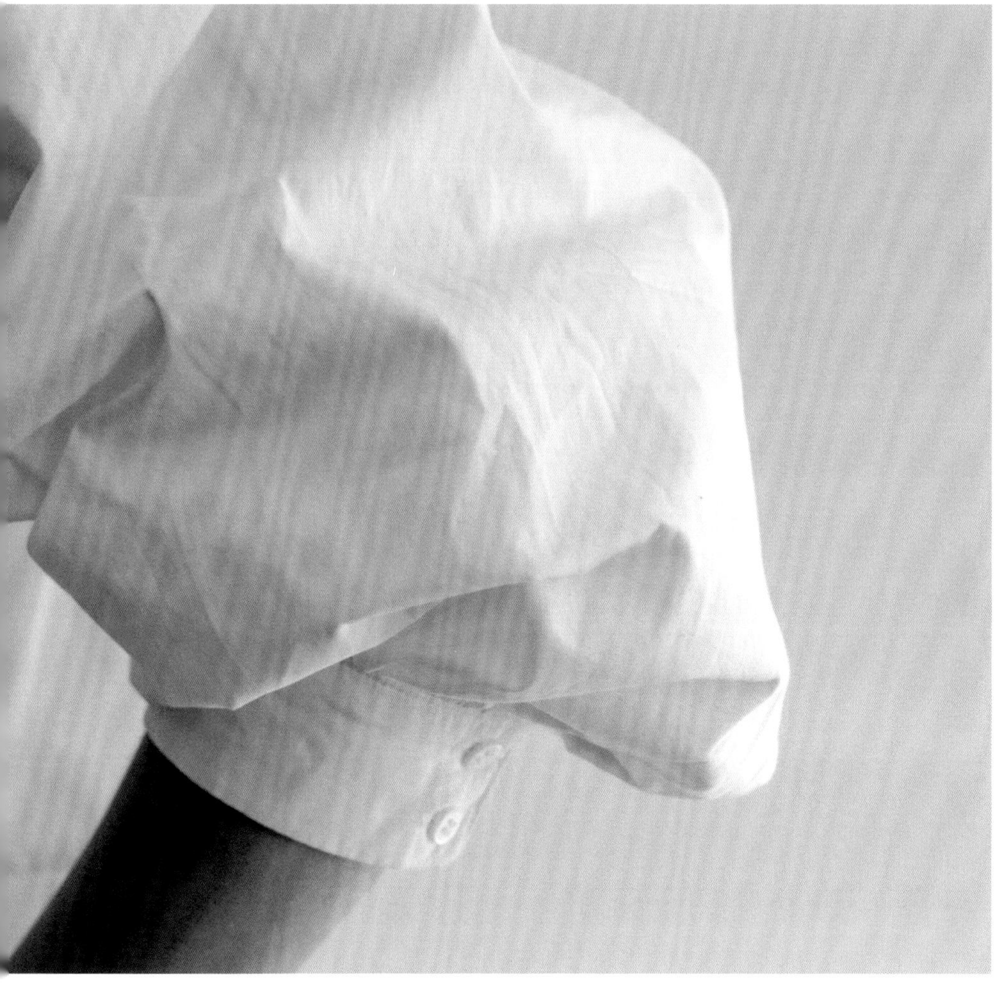

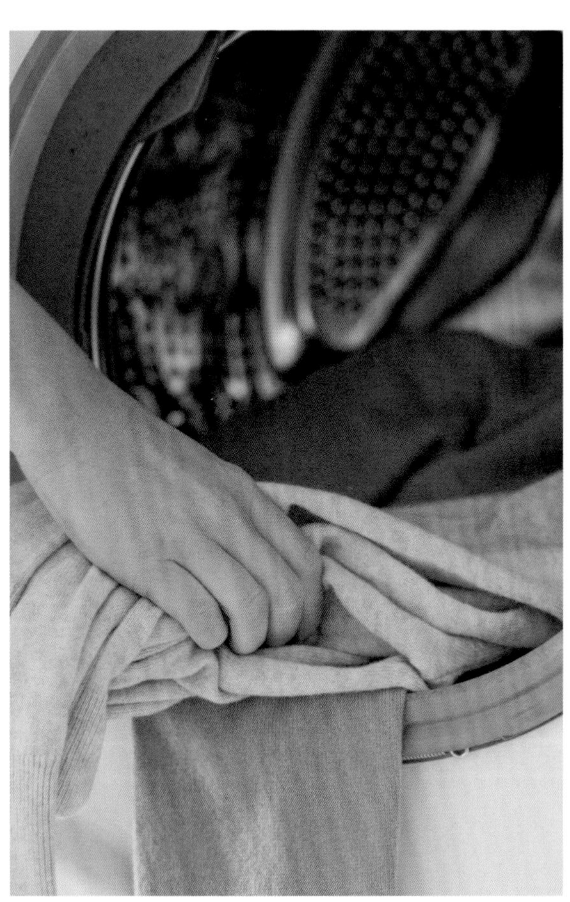

Traditional tools

In most homes you can find a variety of different appliances and gadgets designed to make laundry quicker and easier. But are they good for our clothes?

WASHING MACHINE

Washing machines agitate and spin garments as part of the cleaning process. While modern machines have become more efficient and can wash at lower temperatures, the washing process can be too rough on some fabrics, ripping the fibers and damaging the garment. Eco washing programs prioritize time over temperature and agitation. As clothing is often washed out, not worn out, we recommend you machine wash your clothes as little as possible.

TUMBLE DRYER

Tumble dryers spin wet clothes while blowing hot air through the drum. They can be particularly useful for drying large items such as bed sheets, but the heat and movement in the dryer can cause some fabrics to shrink and tear, damaging them in the long run. Therefore, we don't recommend tumble drying anything but items that can resist a lot of tear.

DRYING CABINET

Wet clothes are hung in a drying cabinet, which gently heats the garments to dry them. While it's a bulkier appliance that uses a lot of energy, it can dry clothes in a much gentler way than the tumble dryer.

IRON AND STEAM IRON

By heating a metal plate and a cartridge of water, clothes can be pressed and steamed to remove unwanted creases. Some ironed garments also get a shiny surface, which is good for items like white business shirts. However, some fabrics are too delicate to be ironed - it's an appliance better suited for heavy fabrics or garments with deep creases.

Alternative tools

STEAMER

A steamer is a tool used to refresh textiles, which not only removes wrinkles but also fights unpleasant odors and bacteria. Steaming is also a smart tool to use when you are traveling and have limited access to laundry facilities. It's generally better to steam delicate fabrics.

FABRIC SHAVER

Electric fabric shavers remove pilling and lint from any kind of clothes or home textiles, collecting the unwanted fuzz in a container.

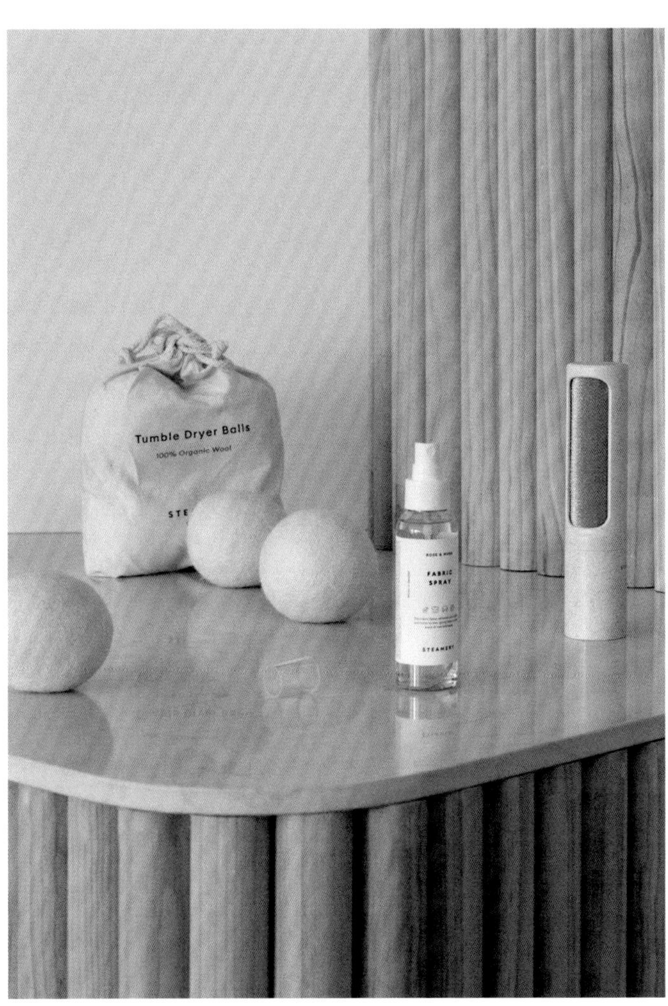
Tumble Dryer Balls
100% Organic Wool
FABRIC
SPRAY
STEAMERY

LINT BRUSH

A lint brush is a reusable alternative to disposable tape lint rollers. The tiny bristles all point in the same direction and catch the lint, hair, dandruff and shallow dirt that collect on fabrics.

FABRIC SPRAY

A fabric spray, or clothing mist, is a good way to refresh clothes that aren't dirty and don't need to be washed yet. They help to disguise bad odors from any type of fabric and make your clothes smell fresh again. A fabric spray also helps to prevent static electricity and future stains as well as softening and smoothing out the fabric.

TUMBLE DRYER BALLS

Tumble dryer balls made of wool are a more sustainable option than most fabric softeners. Simply place them in the tumble dryer together with your clothes and they make your laundry soft and remove static electricity.

Refreshing your clothes without washing

When you've worn a garment once or twice and aren't sure if it needs to be washed yet, it might seem easier to toss it in the laundry basket, just in case. But washing clothes that don't need to go in the laundry is simply a waste of your time and energy. Instead of adding to an overflowing laundry basket, there are lots of simple and quick ways to refresh your clothes without resorting to a washing machine.

There are four main reasons why people wash their clothes unnecessarily – their clothes are creased, stained, have a bad odor or have been worn since they were last washed. Many of us wash garments simply because we don't like to put them back in our wardrobes after they've been used. But clothes should only be laundered when they are dirty. Usually, stains can be spot cleaned without washing the entire garment and bad odors can be aired out, sprayed or steamed away. Here, we suggest some easy alternative methods to washing:

Steaming

Steaming is a great way to quickly revive fabrics and make them feel fresh. The concept of using steam to remove wrinkles has been around since the 19th century and these days technological advances mean steamers have become a must-have appliance for the home. Initially, steamers were more likely to be found in industries such as fashion, theater and costume design. In recent years, however, the popularity of smaller, portable steamers has grown significantly as people have embraced just how quick and easy it is to use a steamer to care for your clothes.

The big difference between steaming and ironing is the way they work to get rid of wrinkles in fabric. Ironing uses a heated metal plate to press out wrinkles, while steaming uses hot steam to relax the fibers in the fabric, allowing them to swell and regain their natural shape so the wrinkles can naturally fall out. While both methods work well against wrinkles, steaming is better for delicate fabrics or garments that are difficult to iron, such as pleated or beaded items of clothing. Steaming is also a quicker and easier process, as it doesn't require a flat surface or as much space as ironing.

Steam removes odors from fabrics by breaking down odor molecules with heat, then carrying them away through moisture. As steam penetrates the fabric, it dislodges and evaporates odor-causing particles, replacing them with fresh moisture. The high temperature of the steam can also sanitize and neutralize certain odors, leaving the fabric refreshed and odor-free.

Not only is steaming good for your clothes, but it's also a mindful, therapeutic act of care that can help you just as much as your garments.

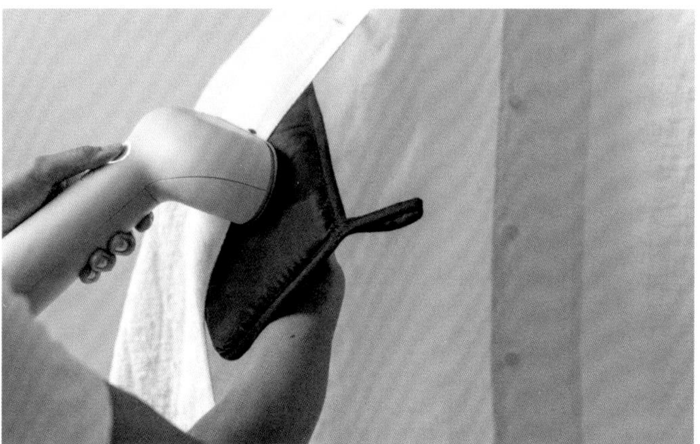

Christopher Bastin, Creative Director at GANT, said: 'I start each collection in the same way, by steaming all the vintage items I've purchased for inspiration and garments from the archive. The calmness that sets in clears the mind.'

STEP 1: FILL THE WATER TANK AND PLUG IN THE STEAMER

Using tap water is fine as long as you have access to soft water. If you live in an area with hard water that is rich in calcium and magnesium, we recommend using special steam water or distilled water as hard tap water can result in limescale residue that will clog the steamer.

STEP 2: PLACE YOUR GARMENT ON A HANGER

Find a place where you can comfortably hang your garment with an electrical outlet nearby – any hook, shower rod or curtain pole will do.

STEP 3: GRAB THE BOTTOM OF THE GARMENT

Gently stretching the fabric while steaming makes it easier to eliminate tough creases.

STEP 4: PRESS THE MOUTHPIECE AGAINST THE FABRIC

Once it is producing steam, move the steamer against the fabric in any direction, top to bottom or sideways.

STEP 5: STEAM FROM THE INSIDE OF THE GARMENT

This is an effective technique for removing creases on button-up shirts, blouses, T-shirts and similar garments.

STEP 6: USE A STEAMING TOOL FOR COLLARS, CUFFS AND HEMS

This can really come in handy when steaming details like collars, cuffs and hems. Simply hold the tool behind the fabric while steaming to create a pressed effect.

Misting

Bad odors are one of the most common reasons why clothes end up in the laundry basket. But if the clothes aren't dirty, why not use a fabric spray or clothing mist instead of washing.

Made with enzymes, probiotics or salts, these sprays help to neutralize or remove the cause of bad odors, making your clothes smell and feel fresh again. A clothing spray is also a perfect travel companion when you are traveling with a limited wardrobe.

Spray directly on the source - such as the armpit of a T-shirt or inside your sneakers - to remove any unwanted odors and make your clothes feel fresh for a little bit longer.

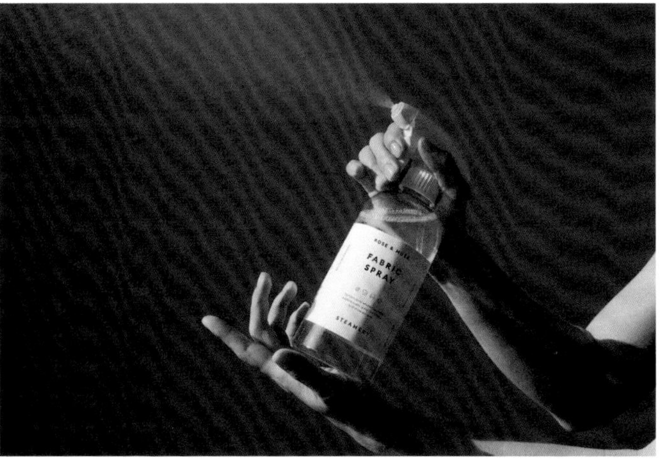

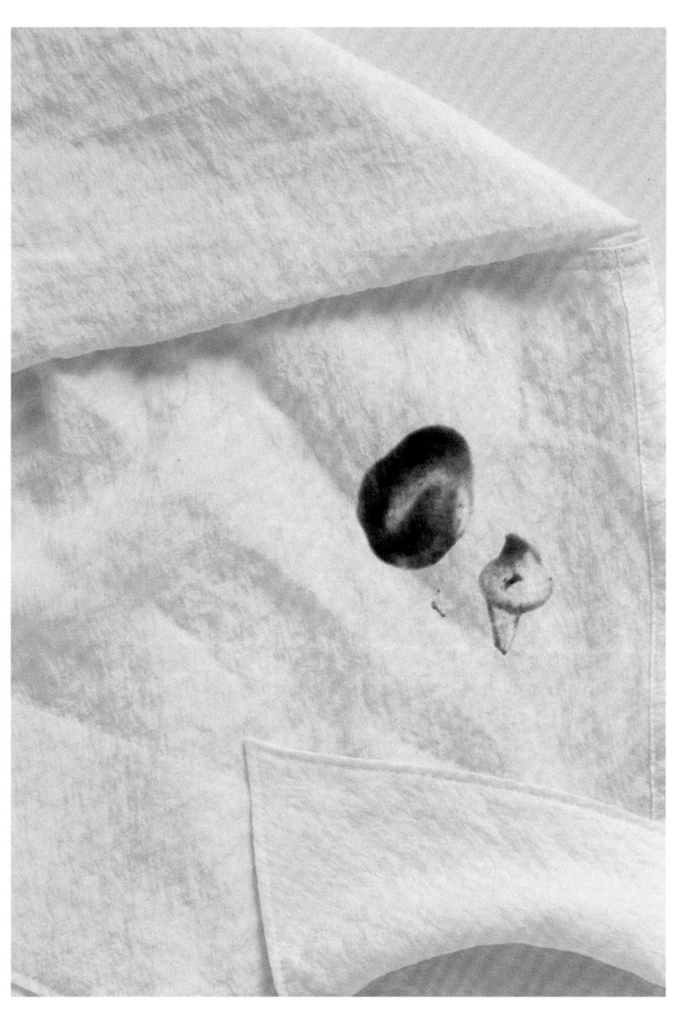

Stain removal

Stain removal is an important way to extend the time between washes and keep your clothes looking their best. What's more, if you can treat the stain when it's fresh, you can eliminate it without having to wash the entire garment.

When a substance is spilled or dropped on a fabric, some of the molecules from that substance become trapped in the fabric, causing the affected material to discolor and take on some of the substance's odor. If you wait too long to treat a stain, it can become really difficult to remove from the fabric – this is because the molecules can harden and 'set' into the fabric.

If left untreated, the stain can damage the fabric over time, as well as harboring bacteria, bad odors and even attracting pests.

There are seven main types of stain remover. It's a good idea to have these at home so you can treat a stain as soon as possible.

DETERGENTS

Detergents typically include surfactants, enzymes and/or soap. These can help to lift stains from your clothes as well as clean them and stop the dirt from re-attaching itself to the textile. For deeper stains, it might be helpful to use another type of stain remover first, then wash your clothes in detergent to ensure the stain is lifted from the fibers.

HYDROGEN PEROXIDE

This is the chemical found in laundry bleach and stain remover powders. A 3 percent solution can do wonders on stains but works best on white clothes. If the stain is on a colored garment, using hydrogen peroxide might bleach away the color as well as the stain.

CITRIC ACID

Citric acid is a natural bleaching agent that reacts with bacteria on your clothes to loosen stains. Like other bleaching agents, it should be used with care on colored garments and is best used on white clothes. It also works well with sunlight to minimize the look of a stain, so it's a good idea to hang your laundry outside to dry if you've used citric acid on a stain.

BILE SOAP

This is soap with bile enzymes, which helps to dissolve fatty stains. It can be used for both white and colored garments and is particularly useful when used on clothes made from natural fibers.

BAKING SODA

This gritty salt reacts with the acidity in some stains to help remove them from fabrics. It also absorbs bad odors and can be used to pretreat a stain. Using it in conjunction with vinegar can help to clean and deodorize your clothes.

VINEGAR

This can be effective for treating stains due to its acidic properties. Vinegar can be useful for treating a wide variety of stains, but it's important to perform a spot test on a small area of the fabric to make sure it doesn't discolor or damage it. It's generally advisable to avoid using vinegar on fabrics sensitive to acid, such as silk or acetate.

BOILING WATER

Boiling hot water was a common way to remove stains in the past. While doing this repeatedly can lead to shrinkage and color loss, pouring boiling water directly through a fabric can have almost magical stain-removing effects.

With these seven stain removers, you will be able to remove even the most stubborn stains. The trick is to remove them as soon as you can and to only treat the area where the stain is located.

If a stain is treated and removed right away (together with a cloth or a little bit of water) there is no need for washing. If the stain is old washing might be needed. Often, fresh stains just need to be treated with a bit of lukewarm water.

Here are some common stains and their remedies:

WINE

Use a stain remover containing hydrogen peroxide. If you don't have any at home, you can sprinkle salt over the stain and let it draw out the moisture for a few minutes, then rinse with hot water. For old wine stains, you can also try using whole milk. Heat the milk until it boils, dip the stain into the milk and let it soak until the milk has cooled.

TOMATO SAUCE

Use a stain remover containing hydrogen peroxide to tackle tomato sauce stains. Make sure to rinse with cold water, as hot water can make the stain permanent. If you don't have any stain remover at home and the stained fabric is white, use a sponge and spot treat the stain gently with lemon juice. Then let it air dry, preferably in the sun. If there are still spots left from the tomato sauce, the sun will act as a natural bleach.

BERRIES

Use vinegar - either white wine or apple cider - and warm water. If you do not have the right vinegar in your pantry, you can also use lemon juice. Apply the vinegar or lemon juice carefully to the stained area and rinse with boiling water, but only if the fabric can handle hot temperatures. If the garment can withstand boiling water, the vinegar isn't necessary.

GRASS

Grass can cause some of the most stubborn stains. The moisture from the grass, along with the chlorophyll, penetrates the textile fibers, which can create permanent stains. The best remedy is to use alcohol, stain remover containing hydrogen peroxide or a gel made with bile soap and sunflower oil. Soak the stain in alcohol, stain remover or gel, then wash the garment on a regular spin cycle at a low temperature. For older stains, use warm water.

BLOOD

To remove fresh blood stains, simply rinse with cold water. For older stains, it is best to use a hydrogen peroxide stain remover. If you do not have a stain remover at home, soak the stained fabric in one tablespoon of salt and 100 ml of water for a couple of hours. Avoid using warm water, as it can make the stain permanent. If the stain remains, mix two parts bicarbonate of soda with one part water, let it soak for half an hour, then brush off the excess and dab with a damp cloth before washing.

MAKEUP

Mix equal parts laundry detergent and baking soda. Apply the mixture to the stain with a clean makeup brush and let it soak for 15 minutes, then wash the garment according to the care label. If it is a severe makeup stain, you can also pre-treat the stain with white spirit to help dissolve it. If the stain remains, treat it with stain remover.

NAIL POLISH

Use a nail polish remover containing acetone. However, always test the product on a small part of the garment first to check the colorfastness before using it on the stain. Soak a cotton pad with the product and dab directly on the stain, then wash according to the care label. We do not recommend this method for synthetic materials, especially not for acetate as acetone can dissolve the fabric.

DEODORANT

Mix two tablespoons of laundry detergent with one tablespoon of citric acid powder. Apply directly on the stain, wait for 30 minutes and rinse with cold water. Another trick to getting rid of deodorant stains is to use vinegar. Mix one part vinegar to ten parts water, let it soak for a few hours, and wash the garment according to the care label.

SELF-TANNING PRODUCTS

Rinse the stain with warm water, then soak the stain with dish soap or liquid laundry detergent. Work the stain from inside the garment, dab gently with a sponge and rinse with warm water. Wash the whole garment according to the care label instructions.

COFFEE

Remove as much of the stain as you can with a piece of kitchen paper. Mix together a solution of one tablespoon of dish soap, one tablespoon of white vinegar and two cups of warm water. Dip a sponge into the solution and blot the stain. Rinse the area with lukewarm water. If the stain is still visible, repeat the process until the stain is removed.

CHOCOLATE

Scrape off any excess chocolate with a knife. Rinse the back of the stain with cold water to flush out as much chocolate as possible. Apply a small amount of liquid laundry detergent directly to the stain and work it into the fabric. Let the detergent work on the stain for at least 15 minutes and rinse. If the stain has not disappeared, apply a stain remover containing enzymes and let it soak for 30 minutes before washing the garment in the washing machine on a gentle cycle. Do not use hot water on chocolate stains as it can set the stain permanently into the fabric.

Pilling

Pilling is something that happens to a range of different textiles but is particularly associated with knitwear. Pills are the little bobbles of fuzz that form at the surface of a textile. Unfortunately, a lot of people think pilling is a sign of bad quality and that garments with pills need to be thrown away, but it's just a natural process that applies to a lot of textiles.

They typically appear where there is frequent abrasion on the fabric, like on the armpits of a knitted sweater or the sleeve of a wool coat. How much pilling a garment will generate depends on certain features of the fabric: knitted fabrics of short and straight fibers and cashmere will generally pill more than others. New garments will also pill more than old, since new clothes have more excess fibers. Knitted fabrics will pill more than woven fabrics as woven fabrics encapsulate the textile fibers and make it harder for them to reach the surface of the garment.

Before considering removing pills it's useful to read the care label as there is a difference between synthetic and natural pills. Synthetic pills are hard to remove, while pills on natural fabrics are easily removed. Synthetic pilling often erupts in loose threads when you try to remove them. Two examples of different materials that pill a lot are acrylic and cashmere.

There are many different ways to remove pilling:

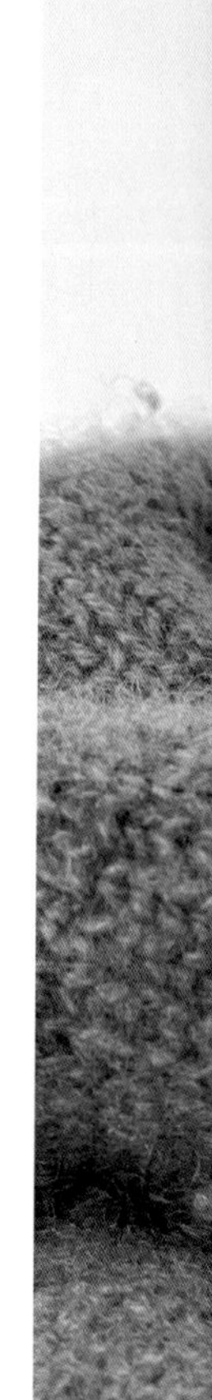

FABRIC SHAVER

A fabric shaver removes pilling and lint from any kind of clothes or home textiles. The machine collects the fuzz in a container that you need to empty every now and then.

In theory, you can use fabric shavers on all textiles. But always be careful and increase the pressure gradually. By gently trying a small part of the fabric you will easily find out if the material is too delicate or not.

To use, remove any leftover lint and fuzz from its last use. Put your garment on a flat surface, press the power button and start circling the areas with pilling carefully.

If you're working on a heavily pilled garment, you might need to check the container and empty it after a while (you will feel and hear when the machine starts to run a little slower).

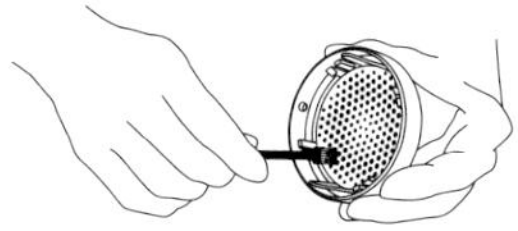

STEP 1: Make sure the fabric shaver has been cleaned properly and remove the leftover lint and fuzz from the last time you used the machine.

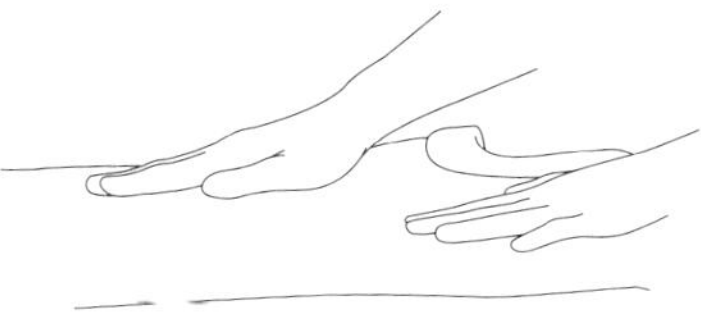

STEP 2: Put your garment on a flat surface.

STEP 3: Press the power button and start circling the areas with pilling carefully.

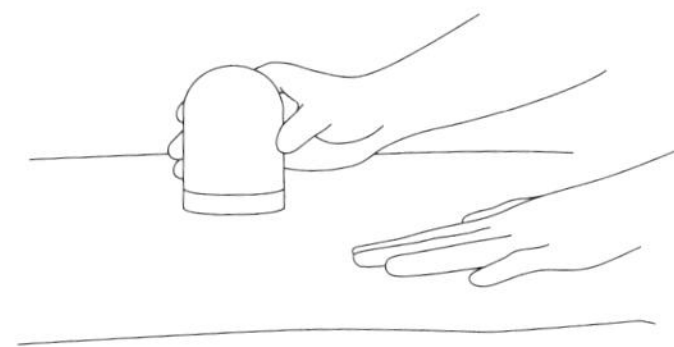

STEP 4: Increase pressure gradually.

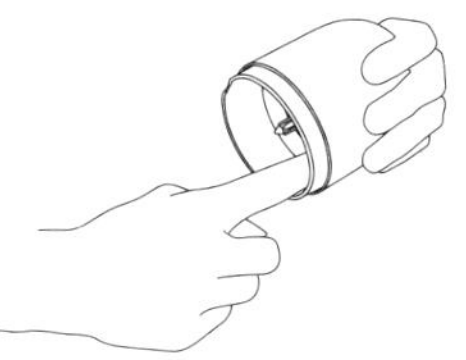

STEP 5: If you're working on a heavily pilled garment, you need to check the container and empty it after a while (you will feel and hear when the machine starts to run a little slower).

DISPOSABLE RAZOR

A razor does the trick for some garments but can be hazardous to others. It's effective against pills on woven fabrics, such as a wool coat with pills around the armpit. But using a razor on knits will destroy them after a few times.

CASHMERE COMB

As the name suggests, this comb is specially designed for cashmere, so it will not remove the hairy surface of the knit.

SPECIALIZED PILL RAZOR

The pill razor is quite interesting and works pretty well on woolen coats and other high-density fabrics. Unfortunately, it will destroy knitted garments and we recommend you use it with care.

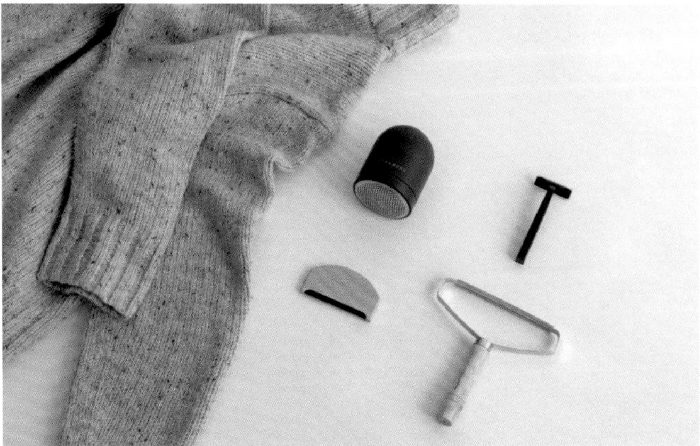

Brushing

Regularly brushing your garments will help to keep them free of superficial dirt that has not penetrated the fabric, including dust, hair and lint. It's particularly useful for reviving jeans or jackets to prolong the time between washes. We've all used disposable sticky lint rollers before, but there are actually reusable lint brushes on the market that are better for your clothes.

Sticky rollers can leave an invisible residue of glue on the garment. As a result, your newly cleaned clothes can become like a magnet for more stuff you don't want on your garments.

You can also find clothing brushes for specific types of fabric - brushes with boar or horse hair bristles are better for delicate items, while copper-wire brushes are good for heavy denim.

Airing

This is the simplest and most natural way of getting rid of odors. Hang your clothes to air out overnight, and they will smell fresh in the morning.

When you hang textiles outside, they are exposed to fresh air and benefit from increased ventilation. This helps remove trapped odors and allows the fibers to breathe, reducing any musty or stale smells. Also, the combination of sunlight, fresh air and wind helps to naturally deodorize textiles.

Sunlight can break down some odor-causing compounds, while the wind carries away airborne particles and helps dissipate any lingering smells.

This trick is effective for all garments made of natural fibers such as cotton, linen, hemp, viscose and wool.

How to wash

When your clothes lose their vibrancy, shape or just look a bit old, it's very rare that they're worn out - they're washed out. Correctly identifying the clothes you really do need to wash can dramatically cut the time and energy you need to spend on laundry.

And when you do need to wash your clothes, it's great to know the right detergents, techniques and temperatures for the clothes in your wardrobe. Essentially, it's all about washing right and washing smart.

Simplifying laundry symbols

It's always good to check the garment's care label before putting an item in the washing machine. Here's our guide to the most common laundry symbols found on care labels. Following these instructions should help to prevent your garments from shrinking or becoming misshapen in the wash.

MACHINE WASHABLE: Any garment with this machine wash symbol is safe to wash in a standard washing machine.

HAND WASH ONLY: Garments with hand wash symbols should only be washed by hand or with a gentle hand wash cycle. If you really love a piece of clothing and have the time, it's more rewarding for you and gentler on the garment to hand wash.

WASH AT MAX. 30°C (85°F): Any garment with this symbol should not be washed with a temperature setting higher than 30°C, otherwise the item might shrink.

WASH AT MAX. 40°C (105°F): Any garment with this symbol should never be washed in temperatures higher than 40°C.

WASH AT MAX. 60°C (140°F): Avoid washing in temperatures higher than 60°C. We would recommend washing at high heat only for items such as linen bed sheets and tablecloths.

 **GENTLE WASH CYCLE:** A washing symbol with two horizontal lines below means that the item can be machine washed, but only if the washing machine has a gentle or wool cycle.

 **NOT MACHINE WASHABLE:** If you see this symbol, always hand wash or dry clean your garment.

Smart washing tips

THE RIGHT DETERGENT

Most people use just the one type of detergent for all their laundry loads, but did you know that your clothes could benefit from being washed in detergent that is specifically tailored for their laundry type? For example, there are detergents made for white clothes that stop your garments from fading and becoming gray. It might not be something you've considered before, but it's definitely worth having a think about next time you're buying more detergent.

THE RIGHT AMOUNT

Being careful about how much detergent you use in each wash can not only keep your clothes looking great, but could also mean you use less for each wash, saving you money. If you use too much detergent in a washing load, your clothes will not get any cleaner. Rather, you're just exposing your clothes to unnecessary chemicals, which may cause damage over time and could leave a residue on the fabric. It's good to read the label on the detergent, which will give you the right dosage instructions. If the detergent comes with a measuring cup or cap, that can often help you to use the right amount.

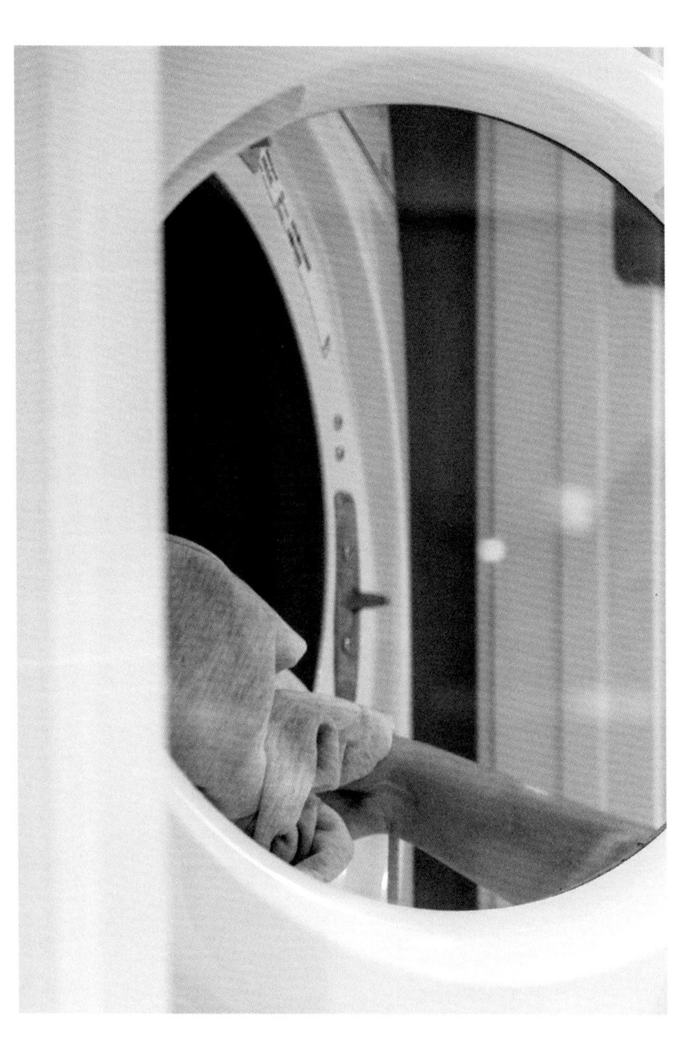

THE RIGHT TEMPERATURE

It's kinder on your clothes to wash at cooler temperatures as hot washes can often cause unnecessary wear and tear. Unless your clothes are heavily soiled or made from more durable textiles, it's usually good to wash at 30°C (85°F). For hygiene reasons, it's advisable to wash your intimate items such as underwear and bedding at a higher temperature setting, such as 60°C (140°F). You may also want to run an empty machine at a high temperature occasionally to prevent the buildup of bacteria. This is because there is always some water left in the machine and bacteria thrive in stagnant, lukewarm water.

THE RIGHT PROGRAM

Why not take a look at your washing machine to see what special programs it offers? For example, if there's a specific wool program, we would recommend you use that for your wool garments. The temperature sometimes changes depending on the program, meaning it's good to remember changing the temperature to 30°C (85°F) before you start the load.

WASHING BAG

Delicate items such as lingerie, bras, hosiery and other items will last longer if they are put in a washing bag before setting a load off. As well as protecting the textiles, it also means they won't get tangled up in other clothes, snagging or stretching. You can even find washing nets, which are specially designed for larger items of clothing such as silk dresses.

NO NEED FOR FABRIC SOFTENER

The good news is if you have access to soft water, you don't need to use fabric softener, which means that's one less thing for you to stock up on. While it can make your garments feel soft, the chemicals inhibit a textile's ability to absorb moisture. If you like your washing to smell especially nice, why not mist it with a fabric spray or air your clothes outside to add extra freshness to your garments?

AIM FOR FULL LOADS

When you have the opportunity, always try to run full loads of laundry. A half-full machine can cause unnecessary wear and tear on clothes. It is also great, from a water and energy perspective, to save the number of times you wash by running full loads instead.

Color-coded loads

Sorting your laundry by color is a good way to prevent discoloration and make sure your garments last for a long time.

We recommend five piles:

1. Black and dark clothes
2. White and light-colored clothes
3. Delicate clothes
4. Red and pink clothes

Alternatively if you need to mix colors it is a good idea to use a color absorber sheet. These small sheets work like magnets, absorbing loose color pigments spinning around in your washing machine, preventing them from being transmitted to other garments. Color absorber sheets are also great for striped or patterned garments with multiple colors.

Using the right detergent

While you might be using just one type of laundry detergent for all your clothes, there are different types of detergent available that cater for specific types of clothes. Here we explain a little more about how each works:

DELICATE TEXTILES

The enzymes in regular detergent are designed to dissolve protein-based stains, but that also means clothes made from natural fibers, such as wool and silk, could be damaged in the wash. A detergent for delicates should therefore not contain enzymes that will dissolve protein-based fibers. Products with added lanolin also moisturize the fibers like a conditioner, making the clothing softer and potentially enhancing its colors.

SPORTSWEAR

Gym clothes have a tendency to get a bit smelly over time. This is because they're usually made out of synthetic fabrics that don't breathe well enough. A sport laundry detergent removes sweaty smells, even the most deeply rooted smells. It's efficient for cleaning all kinds of synthetic garments such as polyester or viscose that will easily attract funky smells.

ROSE & MUSK
DELICATE
Laundry Detergent
WOOL & SILK
STEAMERY
Made in Denmark.

COLOR-SPECIFIC DETERGENTS

The distinction between detergents for dark, white and colored textiles has been a longstanding tradition. Historically, some detergents contained bleach that could damage colors but prove useful for white fabrics.

However, modern detergents are more versatile, effectively handling various stains and preserving colors, which reduces the need for separate whitening detergents. Nevertheless, color-specific detergents still exist for optimal color preservation. These are particularly important for highly dyed items like blue denim. Modern detergents can also work well against graying and help smooth a damage fabric surface.

Liquid or powder detergent

Detergent can come as a powder or a liquid. At Steamery, we recommend you use liquid detergents as they are generally better for your clothes. Liquid detergents are a faster and easier solution in the washing machine and they don't leave a powder residue on textiles. Because they have a lower pH, liquid detergents have better color protection and don't damage fabrics as readily.

Hand washing

If you're especially concerned about keeping your favorite clothes looking their best, then it's a good idea to think about hand washing some of your garments. As we've mentioned already, the twisting and spinning motions of a washing machine can tear and damage the fibers in our clothes, leading to garments becoming prematurely washed out. Hand washing is a much gentler process and the great thing is you have total control of the items you're washing.

It's similar to the idea of hand washing your dishes - while a dishwasher is really useful, there are some special items you wouldn't want to add to a load. And if you can keep your beloved possessions looking great for as long as possible, it's only going to make you feel good too.

Hand washing your clothes can also be an incredibly mindful activity. We encourage you to take the time to slow down, to feel the textures of your garments in the water and to really find a meditative joy in the simple act of caring for your clothes.

Deciding which items you'd consider hand washing really depends on you - as a general rule, all clothes will last longer if they're hand washed. But it's a good idea to check the clothing label as a starting point. If an item is made from a delicate fabric, such as silk, wool, cashmere or merino wool, it will be much better for the garment to be hand washed. Like with detergents for washing machines, always read the label and use the ratio of detergent to water outlined on the bottle.

To hand wash, fill a basin with lukewarm water and then add your chosen detergent. Soak your garment in the mixture and gently work the textile with your hands. Let it rest for 15 minutes and repeat, gently working the water and detergent through the garment, avoiding any harsh rubbing or twisting of the fabric. Once clean, empty the basin and rinse your clothes repeatedly with cold water until there is no detergent residue left.

Once you have washed your clothes, gently squeeze each item to release excess water, but try not to twist the garment. Then, tightly roll the laundry in a terry cloth to release more water. Afterward, gently straighten out the fabric, paying closer attention to the seams, collars and cuffs. Knits should be ideally dried flat - simply lay on a surface and leave to dry. Meanwhile, woven and jersey fabrics work best when they are hung out to dry.

Drying demystified

When caring for your favorite clothes, the process of drying right is just as important as washing. If you dry without considering the type of fabric or material, you could end up with garments that have shrunk or become misshapen.

There is a variety of ways to dry your clothes and the best place to start is by looking at the care label.

Drying symbols explained

TUMBLE DRYING ALLOWED: A plain tumble-drying symbol simply means that the item is made to withstand being dried in a tumble dryer.

TUMBLE DRY ON THE GENTLE PROGRAM: Some tumble dryers will have gentle programs for delicate items. If you don't find this option, choose the lowest possible heat level to minimize wear and tear, and remove your items promptly.

TUMBLE DRY ON THE HIGH PROGRAM: This symbol would typically be found on items that are made to withstand higher temperatures, like sheets or tablecloths.

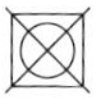

NO TUMBLE DRYING: Never tumble dry items with this symbol. Most garments with this symbol will be harmed or shrunk when dried in a tumble dryer due to the heat and rigorous movements. Hang dry, air dry or flat dry these garments to help them last longer.

HANG DRY: If you see this symbol, let your garment line dry in the air without any added heat. Most garments will last longer and keep their shape if you let them slowly dry on a drying rack or on a hanger.

DRIP DRY: A square icon with three vertical lines inside means your garment should be drip dried. Not to be confused with hang drying, drip drying is when you hang the item in your shower to dry, allowing excess water to drip down the drain.

FLAT DRY: Some items of clothing, like knitted garments, should be flat dried to maintain their shape. Place the garment on a towel, roll it up and carefully squeeze out any excess water. Then lay it flat and leave it to dry.

DRY CLEAN ONLY: Garments with this symbol could be ruined when exposed to water. Bring this garment to your nearest dry cleaner, preferably one with a more environmentally friendly profile.

DO NOT DRY CLEAN: Garments with this symbol on the care label can be easily damaged by solvents used in dry-cleaning processes.

Drying techniques

AIR DRY: Most garments will last longer and keep their shape if you let them slowly dry on a drying rack or on a hanger. Make sure to straighten hems and creases as much as possible, this will save you time when you want to steam the dry clothes.

FLAT DRY: Dry your knitted garments on a flat surface to help them keep their shape. Place the garment on a towel, roll it up and carefully squeeze out any excess water. Then lay it flat and leave it to dry. If you use a drying rack, use a towel as a base to prevent creasing. If your knitted garment is quite bulky, it's good to flip it when the upper half is dry.

TUMBLE DRY: While tumble drying is quick and easy, the heat and movement can shrink, misshape and harm your clothes and textiles. The fuzz you have to remove from the tumble dryer is actually textile fibers ripped prematurely from the fabric. At Steamery, we would recommend avoiding the tumble dryer, apart from when drying bed linen and towels. But, if you're short of time and need to use it for more general laundry, adding tumble dryer balls to the drum can shorten the drying time and remove the static electricity.

Saving a shrunken sweater

What do you do when disaster strikes and you've accidentally shrunk an sweater in the wash? It can be a frustrating experience, especially if it's a cherished sweater. Luckily, there are a few methods you can try to unshrink a sweater and restore it to its original size.

SOAK IN LUKEWARM WATER

Let the sweater soak in baby shampoo and lukewarm water for half an hour. The baby shampoo will soften the fibers of the sweater and make it easier to stretch back to its original size. If you don't have baby shampoo, delicate detergent could be a good alternative.

GENTLY STRETCH THE FABRIC

After soaking the sweater for about 30 minutes, rinse thoroughly and gently stretch it out to its original size. Be careful not to pull too hard, as this can cause the fibers to break or damage the sweater. Instead, gently work the sweater back into its original shape.

STEAM OR PRESS THE SWEATER

Once the sweater is dry, a steamer will really help to reshape it. Put the sweater on a sturdy hanger and work through the whole garment while continuing to gently stretch the fabric evenly in all directions. Hopefully your sweater will be saved and can be used for many years to come.

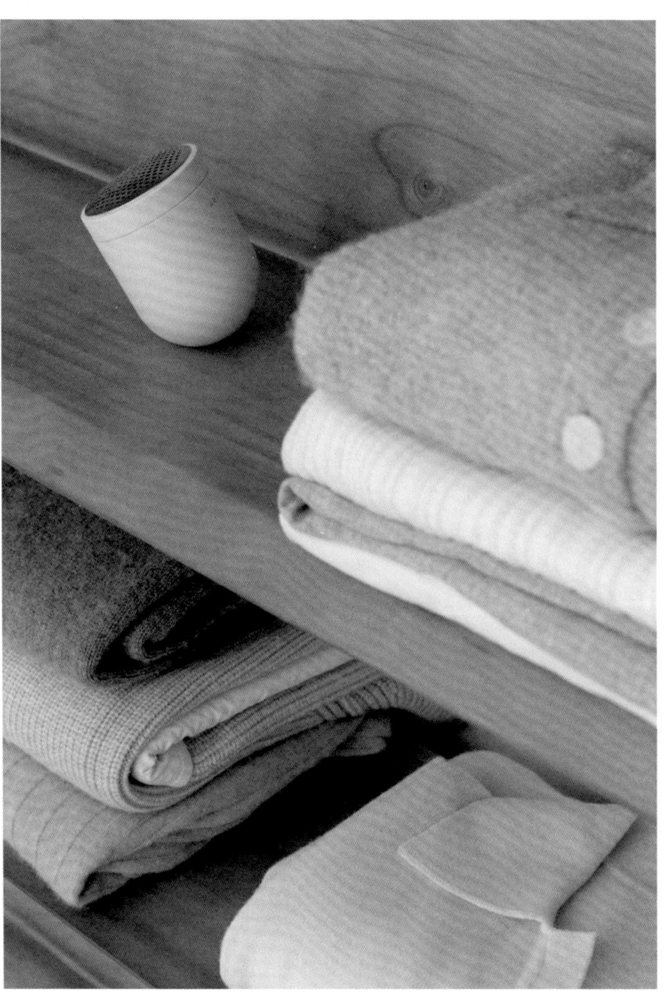

Storage

The way you store your clothes is important if you'd like your most-loved garments to always look their best. It may feel like it's easier to toss your clothes on a nearby chair when you're done with them, but it only takes a few seconds more to tidy them away properly. What's more, storing your clothes in a caring way will make you feel more organized and able to pick out outfits more easily.

It's important to ensure the garment is completely dry before storing it, as any residual moisture can lead to mold or mildew growth during storage.

It's also a good idea to steam your garment once it's properly dried. This helps to remove wrinkles, eliminate mild odors, prevent pests and restore your garment's shape. Once steamed, allow the garment to air dry thoroughly before placing it in your closet or storage container.

HANG OR FOLD?

Putting away your clothes correctly can help them to retain their shape and stay in good condition for longer. When you're tidying clothes away, think about whether the garment might pull, or be too heavy to be hung up. Knits and sweaters should be folded, while coats and jackets should be stored on hangers.

HANGING CLOTHES: Use padded or wooden hangers to maintain the garments' shape. Avoid overcrowding the closet to prevent wrinkles and damage. Use garment bags to protect delicate fabrics like silk and beaded garments from dust and snags.

KNITWEAR: Fold knitted garments to prevent them from stretching or getting hanger marks.

DELICATE FABRICS: Store delicate fabrics, such as silk and chiffon, in garment bags to protect from dust and sunlight. Avoid hanging delicate fabrics, as they can stretch. Instead, fold them carefully.

LEATHER AND SUEDE: Store in a cool, dry place away from direct sunlight to prevent fading and drying out. Avoid using plastic bags, as they can trap moisture. Use cloth or paper bags for protection.

DENIM: Fold denim items to maintain their shape and avoid stressing the seams. It's also best to store them away from direct sunlight to prevent fading.

FORMAL WEAR: Use padded hangers or specialty garment bags to protect intricate details and prevent wrinkles on evening gowns and tuxedos.

ACCESSORIES: Hang scarves and belts on hooks or racks to prevent creasing. Store hats on shelves or in hat boxes to maintain their shape.

Seasonal storage

If you're rotating your wardrobe seasonally or need to pack clothes away in long-term storage, there are a few tips to keep in mind to make sure your garments stay in their best condition.

Before packing the clothes away, giving each item a steam can help to remove wrinkles and odors, as well as sanitizing the garment before it is stored. It's best to keep your clothes in a spot with low humidity, since damp air can make your clothes grow mold. If you're putting boxes of clothes in storage, places like an attic or a heated garage can be great.

If you are storing your clothes away for a long time, you can also buy special vacuum bags. These bags will keep your clothes free of dust, moths and moisture. Use them if you have experienced problems with vermin or if you're looking for a smart way to save space.

Clean and properly store off-season clothes in breathable containers, away from moisture and pests.

Remember to clean garments before storing them for an extended period, as stains can set over time. Additionally, avoid using mothballs, which can be harmful and have a strong odor. Instead, consider using natural alternatives like lavender sachets or cedar blocks.

Pest control

Pests, such as moths and carpet beetles, can destroy natural textile fibers, which can be a particular concern when storing items for a long time. Thankfully, there are a few ways to protect your clothes from these pests. As a general rule, it's best to avoid storing dirty or smelly garments as this can attract vermin.

It's a good idea to store each garment in a cotton or plastic bag. This will keep them out of reach for any vermin.

Why not mist your clothes with cedar-wood oil or store them with blocks or balls or rings made of cedar wood? Moths and fur beetles are repelled by the sharp smell of cedar. If you are using cedar blocks, make sure to scrape the surface of the wood occasionally to keep spreading the scent.

Trickier garments

Most of us own clothes that are extra special to us, like a wedding dress, a tailored suit or a wool coat. All these garments need some special treatment to last as long as we want. Let's look at some garments that might feel difficult to take care of.

BEADED, EMBROIDERED AND PLEATED GARMENTS: It's best to always hand wash garments that have delicate details such as beading and embroidery. But if the care label says you can machine wash the garment, put it in a washing bag and set it on a gentle cycle at a low temperature to ensure none of the stitching comes undone or any beads are pulled off. After washing, we would recommend air drying then steaming the garment.

MULTI-COLORED APPAREL: When washing multi-colored garments, it's always helpful to use a color absorber sheet. Washing with a color detergent on a colder setting will also help to prevent the colors from running too much.

PRINTS: Printed T-shirts can often age badly if cared for in the wrong way. To protect the printed artwork, turn your T-shirt inside out before putting it in the wash, and make sure you set your washing machine on a cooler setting. It's best to avoid tumble drying, as the heat can degrade the print. If ironing the T-shirt, it's best to place a tea towel between the garment and the iron so it doesn't melt or remove any of the design.

SUITS: Most suits should never be washed in the machine due to shrinking or losing shape. If your suit has caught an unpleasant odor, try to air it out overnight, steam it and mist it with a lightly scented fabric spray. If this doesn't work, check to see if it can be hand washed or sent to a dry cleaner.

DOWN JACKETS: The 'wash less' rule is definitely applicable to down jackets. In fact, frequent washing can easily result in the down losing its fluffiness. Down jackets can also really benefit from some air circulation to remove odors. When washing, opt for a delicate detergent or detergent made for down apparel, choose a gentle cycle and wash at a low temperature. If you choose to tumble dry your down jacket, let it dry inside out at a low temperature. Adding tennis balls to the tumble dryer will help preserve fluffiness. If you prefer not to use a tumble dryer, you can lay the jacket flat on a drying rack in a well-ventilated area. Make sure to fluff the down and shift it around occasionally to prevent clumping.

COATS OR WINTER JACKETS: To keep your coats and jackets fresh between washes, make a habit of brushing and occasionally spritzing them with some fabric spray. If your jacket is made of a natural material, you can simply hang it outside to air overnight to make it feel fresh again. When you do wash your jackets or coats, check the care label first. If they can be hand washed, use a detergent made for delicate fabrics.

WEDDING DRESS: Steam your wedding gown with a steamer to make it wrinkle-free and smooth as a last step before the ceremony. But be careful and always try on a small surface first to make sure your delicate dress won't get any stains or marks from the water or heat. After the wedding, the main aim is to clean and preserve your wedding dress. Take the garments to the dry cleaner as quickly as possible after the wedding. Also hang the dress on a padded hanger that is much gentler than a wire or wood hanger. If the dress is heavy, store it laying down flat. Store your dress or suit in a dry, cool, and dark place, in a fabric bag designed for garment storage.

SHELL JACKETS: The good thing about shell jackets is that dirt tends to stay on the surface. Most of the time you can therefore use a clothing brush to sweep off dirt or dust. When you need to wash your shell jacket, wash on low temperatures and use a laundry detergent recommended for shell jackets. To maintain the waterproofing, you may have to re-impregnate your jacket. Choose a spray that is free from PFCs (substances that are dangerous to animals and humans, and aren't biodegradable) and, most preferable, ECO-labeled.

SWIMWEAR: Swimwear should never be machine washed, a gentle hand wash in cold water is enough. Use laundry detergent made for sportswear to remove any sour smells. Rinse your swimwear carefully with fresh water after every use. Also remember that sunscreen stains can turn yellow and be extremely stubborn to get rid of. Try to apply sunscreen and let it absorb before putting on your swimwear. When re-applying sunscreen, try not to let it touch your swimwear.

At Steamery, we believe clothing care can be quick, easy and fulfilling. By making small changes to your clothing care routine, you can show your garments the love they deserve and take inspiration from the small moments when we are able to slow down - whether that's while hand washing a much-loved item or while steaming a garment.

We encourage you wash less, reclaiming time and energy from loading and unloading the washing machine, instead taking the time to care for your wardrobe in the way your clothes deserve.

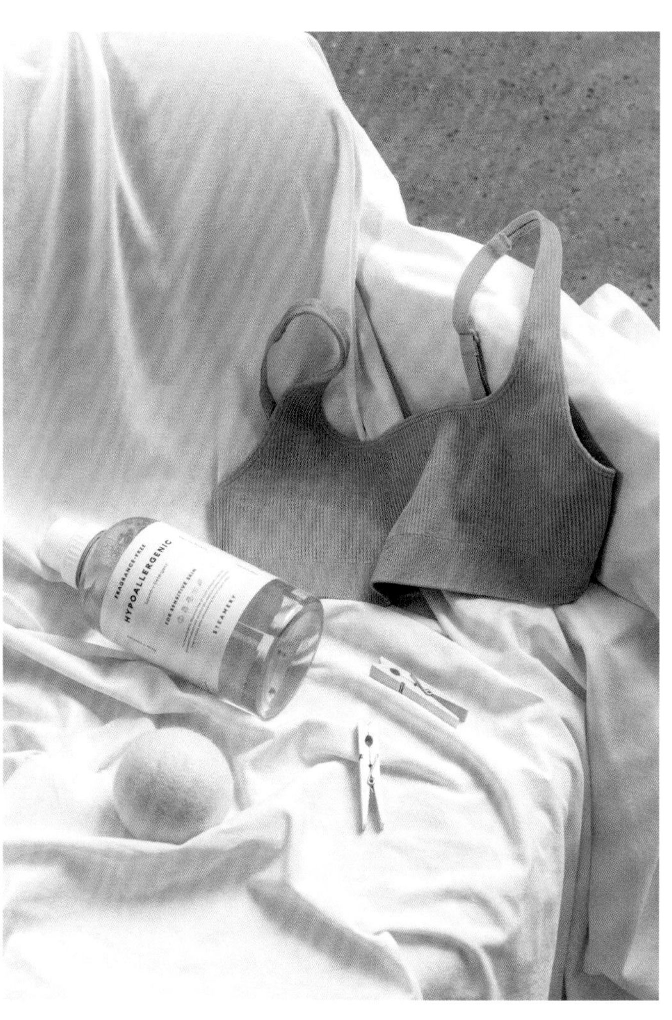
FRAGRANCE-FREE
HYPOALLERGENIC
FOR SENSITIVE SKIN
STEAMERY

CHAPTER 3

MAKE DO AND MEND

Many of us throw away items of clothing just because of a ripped seam or a missing button. But instead, you could repair your clothes so they can continue to be worn and loved for generations.

In the past, easy mending and patching were common habits in all homes. Clothes were tailor-made and relatively more expensive, so people simply mended and altered their clothes until they were no longer usable. As the clothing industry began manufacturing clothes it became cheaper and more accessible to buy new garments. As a result, even the most common mending knowledge has been lost by many.

In this chapter we will teach you the basics of mending and how to upcycle clothes you may think have reached the end of their life cycle. With the right tools and guidance, mending damaged clothes is an easy and enjoyable routine that could help your clothes last longer.

With these skills, you'll be able to keep your favorite garments looking great, as well as reinvent items to better reflect your style and personality. Mending is an incredible act of craftsmanship and it can be very mindful and fulfilling to care for your favorite clothes yourself. By putting time and energy into caring for your clothes, you are caring for yourself. So, why not pick up a needle with us and learn some simple tricks to tailor your wardrobe to you?

The beginner's sewing kit

It's always quicker and easier to mend clothes if you have some sort of sewing kit at home. But, if you're new to repairing your own clothes, don't worry about getting a full set immediately – you can do most easy mends with just a couple of items. It's really useful to have a small sewing kit close to hand so you can quickly grab it whenever you need to mend or alter your clothes.

We recommend starting with a smaller project before taking on more complex repairs. Take your time and allow yourself to build in confidence until you feel more comfortable sewing.

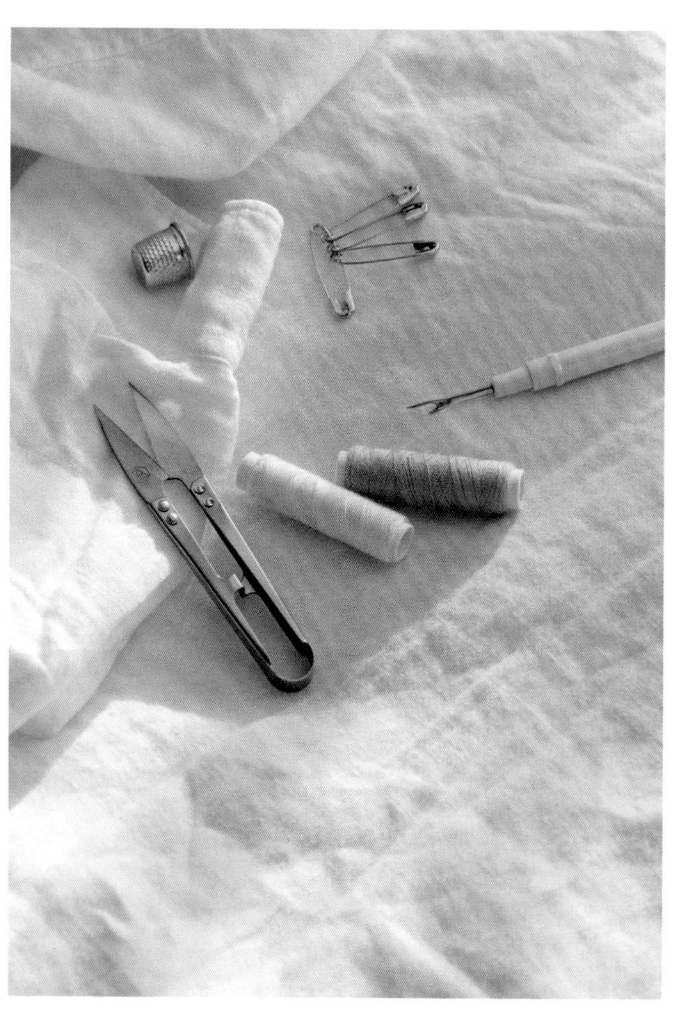

What you need for basic mending by hand

- Thread (start off with just a few colors, such as white, black and dark blue)
- Needles
- Scissors suitable for cutting fabrics
- Seam ripper

When you feel more confident

- Sewing machine
- Thimble
- Quick patches
- Buttons
- Measuring tape
- Pins
- Fabric pen
- Needle threader
- Darning egg

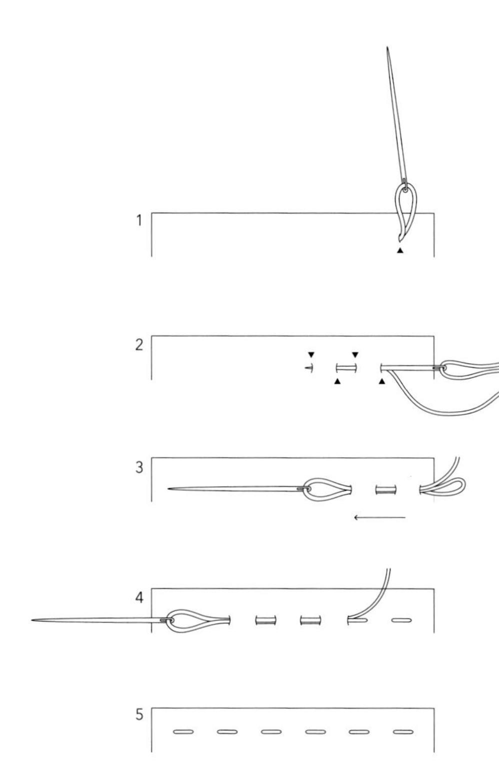
1
2
3
4
5

Sewing techniques

There is a jungle of sewing techniques out there. So, which ones do you actually need to know about? Here are five of the most common stitching methods, all of which are useful when you are new to mending:

BASTING STITCH

Basting stitches are long and loose stitches used to hold fabric pieces together temporarily while sewing a seam or attaching a zipper. Basting stitches are easily removed once the permanent stitching is finished. They are particularly useful when working with slippery fabrics that can shift during the sewing process. It's similar to pinning fabrics but it is a more secure method and means you won't be poked by pins while you work.

LADDER STITCH

Ladder stitch, also known as invisible stitch or slip stitch, is a technique used to fix holes in seams without leaving visible stitches. To use ladder stitch, start by turning the fabric edges inward to create a neat edge. Then, knot the thread and bring the needle up through one side of the fabric, taking it straight across the gap to the other side. Sew a small stitch in the fabric and take the needle back across the gap, insert it into the opposite side and take it diagonally across to the first side. Continue this process, making small stitches and pulling the thread tightly to create an invisible seam.

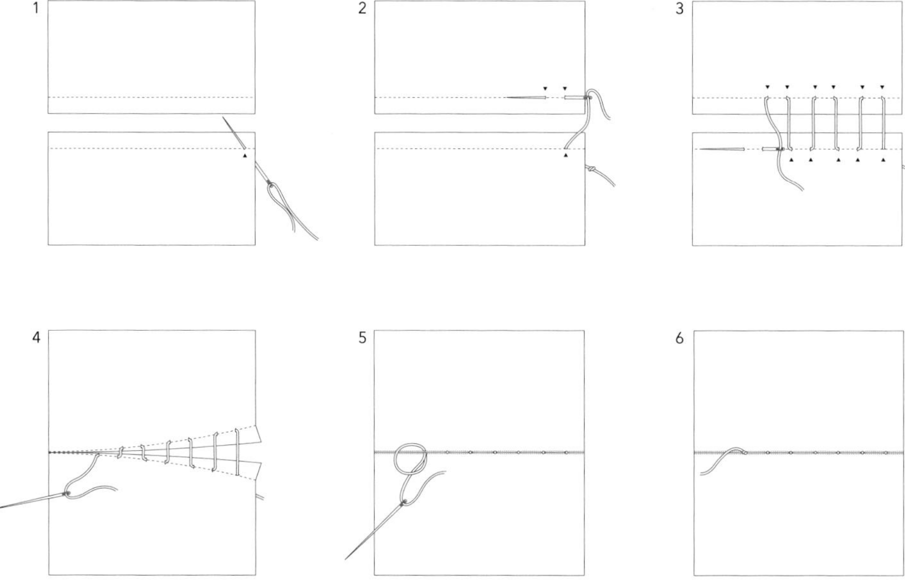

WHIP STITCH

A whip stitch is a simple stitch used to sew two pieces of fabric together. It involves taking the needle up and down through the fabric, creating a series of loops that secure the edges together. It is great for edges, seams or hems. Make the stitches close together to prevent fraying.

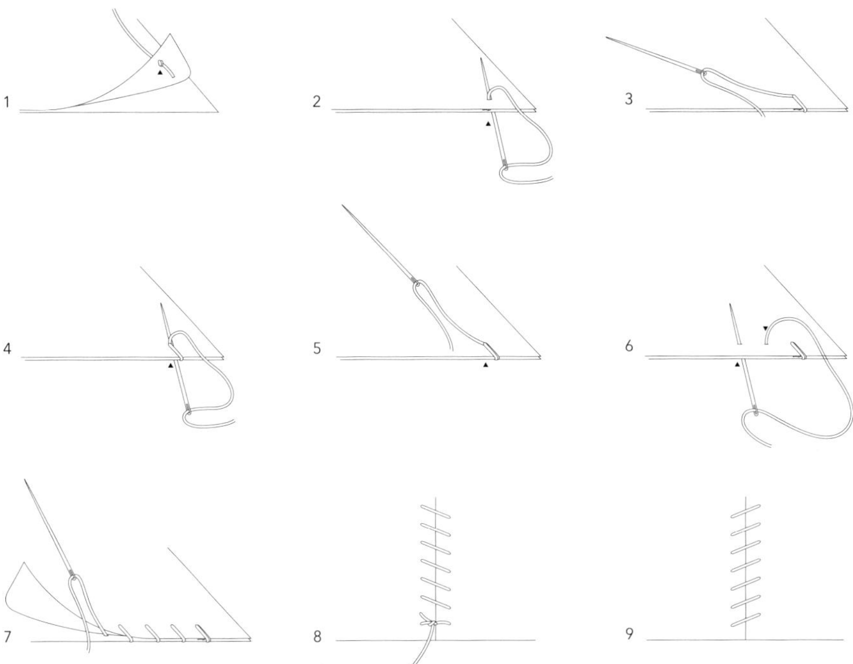

RUNNING STITCH

Running stitch, also known as a straight stitch, is a basic stitch where the thread simply passes in and out of the fabric in a straight line. It is a quick and easy stitch often used in embroidery to create outlines and for the Japanese embroidery technique sashiko.

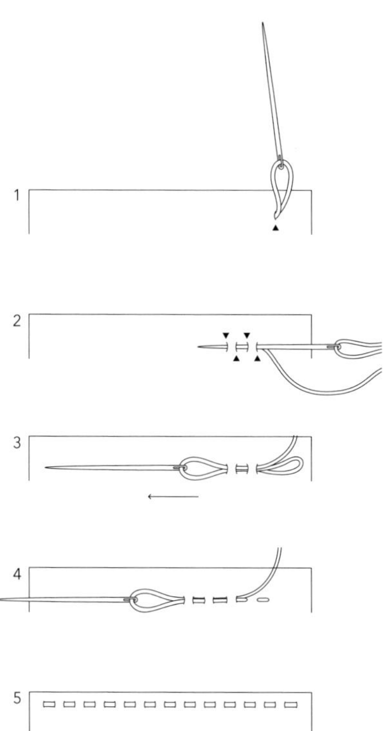

BLANKET STITCH

Blanket stitch is a decorative diagonal stitch that is commonly used to finish the edges of blankets and other fabric items. To use blanket stitch, start by knotting the thread and bring the needle up through the fabric from the back. Thread over the edge of the fabric and insert it back into the fabric at a diagonal angle, creating a loop on the edge of the fabric. Continue this process, pulling the thread tight to create a neat and even edge.

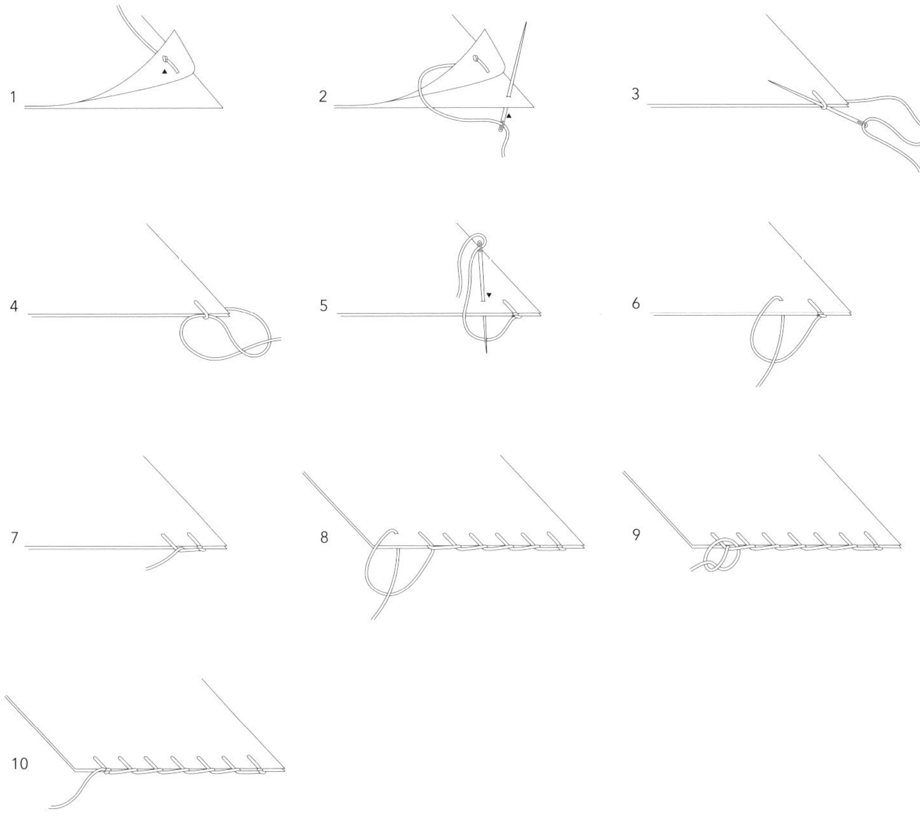

Hand sewing vs. machine sewing

Hand sewing and machine sewing are two different methods and there are several pros and cons for both of them. It's important to choose the method that works best for your project and personal preferences.

SPEED: Machine sewing is much faster than hand sewing. A sewing machine can stitch several feet of fabric in just a few minutes, while hand sewing requires more time and patience.

PRECISION: A sewing machine can produce very precise stitches, while hand sewing may not be as consistent or accurate.

SKILL LEVEL: Machine sewing requires a certain level of knowledge. Hand sewing can be learned by anyone with a basic needle and thread.

COST: A sewing machine can be a significant investment, while hand sewing only requires a few basic tools such as needles, thread and scissors.

PORTABILITY: Hand sewing can be done anywhere, while machine sewing requires a power source and a stable surface.

CREATIVITY: Hand sewing allows for more creativity and control over the stitching process. With hand sewing, you can stitch unique patterns, add decorative touches and repair small areas with more precision.

Thread a needle like a pro

USE GOOD LIGHTING: Make sure you are in a well-lit area. It can make all the difference.

WET THE END OF THE THREAD: This is a well-known sewing hack that will make it easier to thread through the needle's eye.

USE A NEEDLE THREADER: This is a really helpful tool if you are struggling to thread the needle. Insert the thread through the needle threader's wire loop, then pull the needle threader through the needle's eye.

TIE A KNOT: Tie a knot at the end of the thread to help it stay in place when sewing. How big a knot depends on the fabric. Pull the needle and thread through the garment and see if it slips through or not. If yes, you need to make a bigger knot.

DON'T WASTE THREAD: If you hate threading needles, a longer thread is better but remember that less is more and only use what you need. A thread that is too long can tangle and be in the way when sewing.

Double threading

A double thread is used to make a stronger stitch by taking two strands of thread and threading them through the needle together.

Simply cut a length of thread that is twice the length you would normally use and thread the needle. Pull it through until you have two even strands. Tie a knot at the end to secure.

If you're using a sewing machine, read the manual to find out how to double thread for your particular machine.

Darning

Darning is a sewing technique often used when repairing holes in knits or other fabrics. Simply use a needle and thread to weave new threads into the hole, filling it. Darning is often done by hand but can also be done with a sewing machine. For the best result, use a darning needle with a large eye and a thicker yarn like sashiko thread or embroidery thread.

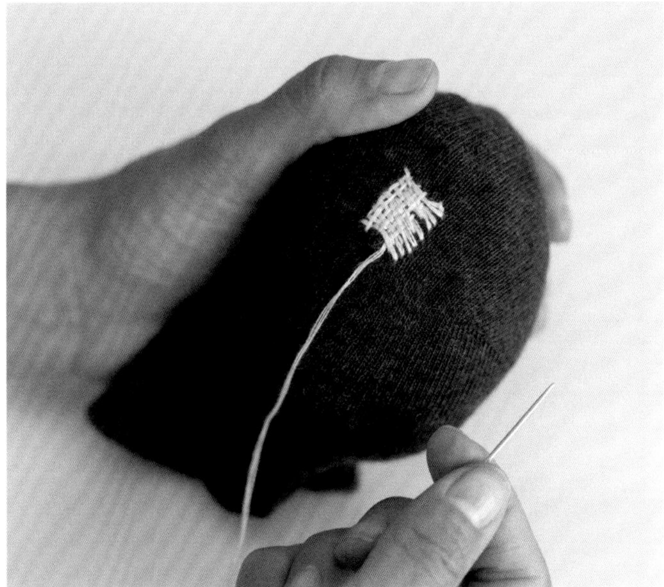

Sashiko

Sashiko is a traditional Japanese embroidery technique that involves using a running stitch to create decorative and functional patterns on fabric. The word 'sashiko' means 'little stabs' in Japanese, referring to the small stitches that are used in the technique.

To use sashiko, you will need the following materials:

Fabric (traditionally, indigo-dyed cotton)
Sashiko thread (a thick, cotton thread)
Sashiko needle (a long, straight needle with a large eye)
Sashiko template (optional)

STEP 1: Firstly, choose a sashiko design or create your own template.

STEP 2: Thread your needle with sashiko thread, leaving a tail of thread that is about the length of your arm. Knot the end of the thread and begin stitching from the back of the fabric, following the design you have chosen.

STEP 3: Use a running stitch to create the design. Make sure to leave the same amount of space between each stitch. When you reach the end of the thread, attach it and begin again with a new thread.

STEP 4: Continue stitching until your design is complete.

Sashiko can be used to embellish a variety of fabric items including clothing, accessories and home decor items. The technique can also be used for visible mending and patching, creating a decorative and functional repair on damaged clothing or textiles.

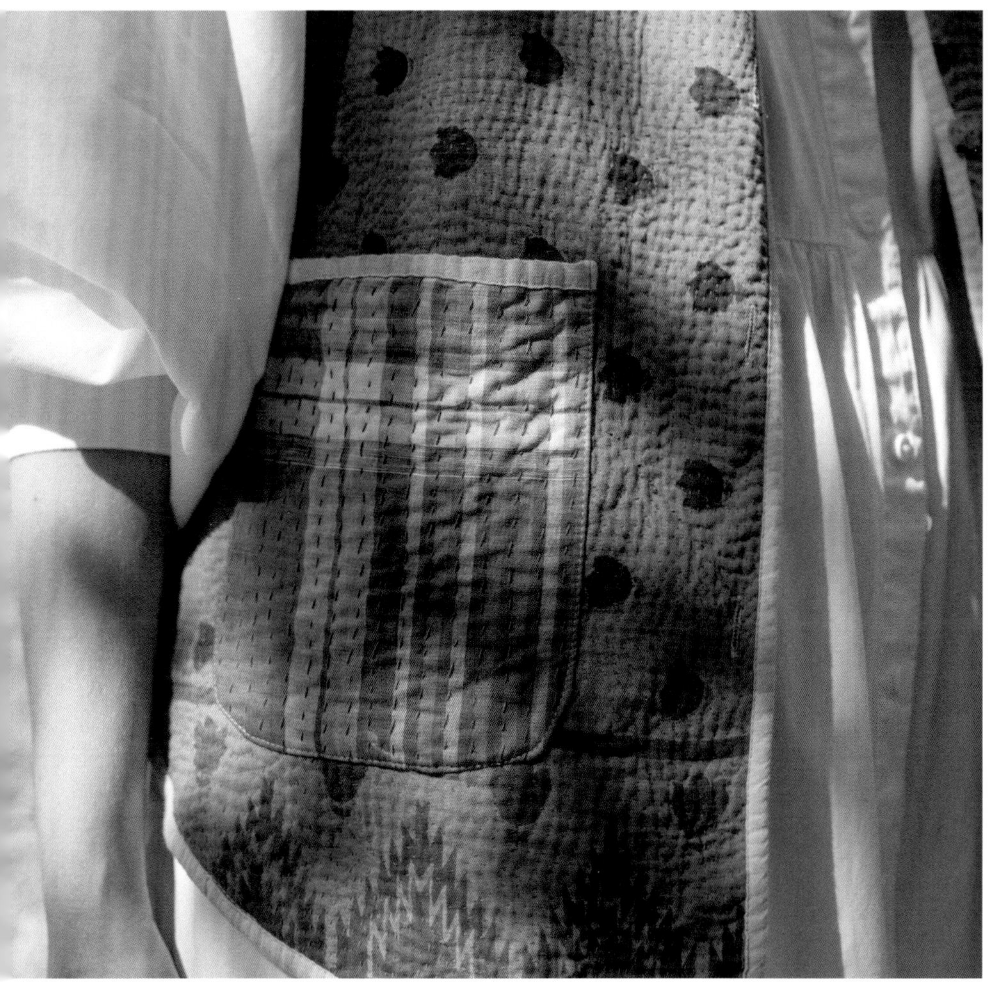

How to repair your clothes

We have gathered some common repairs and the mending methods used to fix them in our easy step-by-step tutorials. Grab your sewing kit and start practicing.

Before you start, it's good to think about the color of the thread. If you want to hide the thread in the fabric but can't find a perfect color match, choose a thread that is slightly darker in color rather than lighter. Light colors will stand out much more.

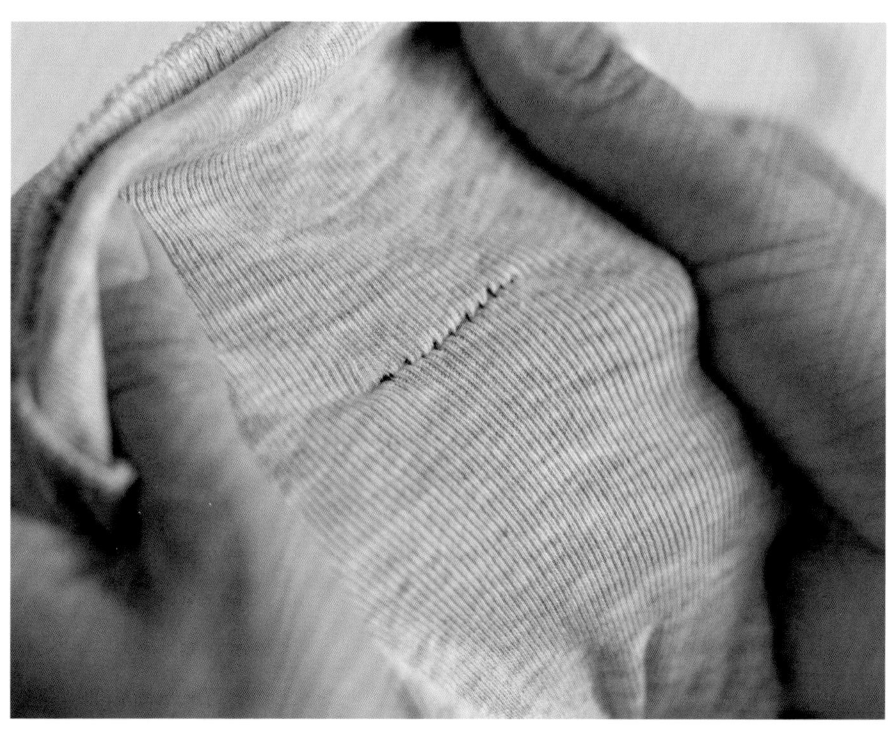

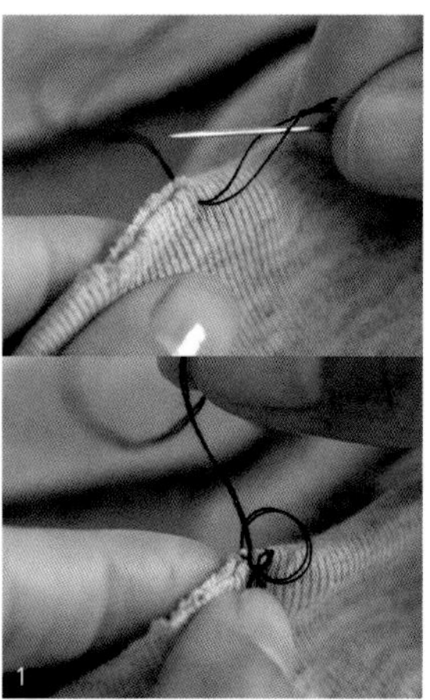
1

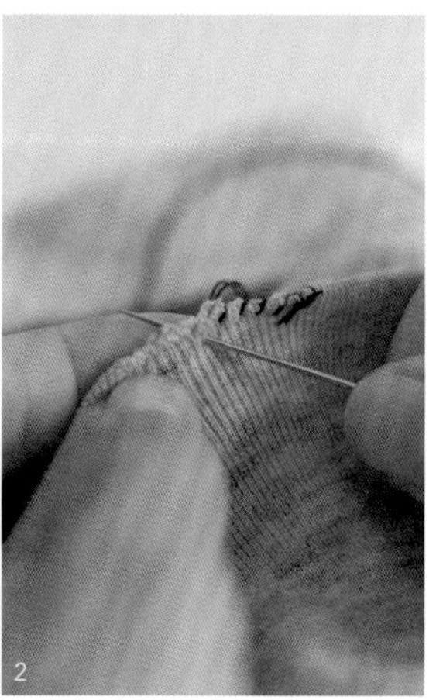
2

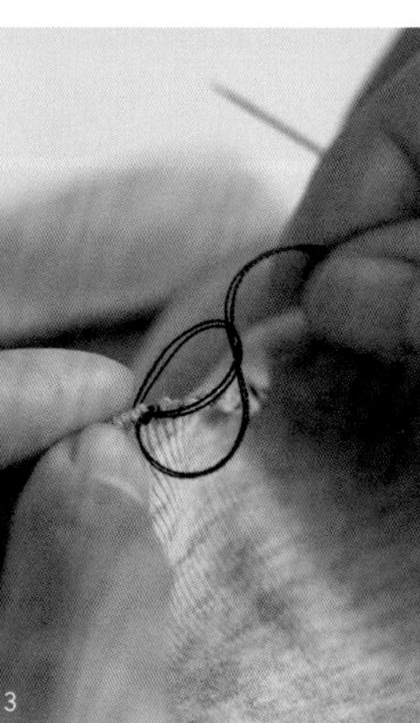
3

Holes

Holes are one of the most common repairs that need to be made on everyday garments such as denim, cotton shirts or knits. With the help of a needle and a thread you can quickly and easily make these garments whole again.

A SMALL HOLE

With tiny holes or tears in a garment, there is no need to use a patch. These holes can easily be fixed with just a few quick stitches. To make your repair as subtle as possible, choose a thread that closely matches the color of the fabric.

You'll need:
Thread
Needle

STEP 1: Thread the needle and tie a knot at the end of the thread. Insert it next to the hole from the inside of the garment. Attach the thread by sewing three stitches on top of each other. Test that it is steady by gently pulling the thread.

STEP 2: Sew a few stitches across the hole. Remember to insert the needle a bit away from the torn edge so that the fabric does not rip open. Sew as many stitches as needed to make the hole disappear.

STEP 3: Attach by threading the needle under a stitch on the back a couple of times.

LARGER HOLES

A larger hole is commonly fixed with a patch. You can either use a ready-made patch or cut your own patch out of a piece of cloth. Choose a patch that matches the color and material of the garment, or why not add a pop of color? This is an opportunity to get creative.

You'll need:
Thread
Needle
Scissors
Patch

STEP 1: If you're cutting a patch from a piece of fabric, start by cutting it out, then zigzag the edges and fold them under. The patch should cover with hole with a margin of 1 cm larger all around it.

STEP 2: Pin the patch, or secure it with a few temporary basting stitches, then thread a needle and tie a knot at the end of the thread. Sew the patch on with your chosen stitch technique.

STEP 3: Attach the thread with a few stitches on the inside of the garment.

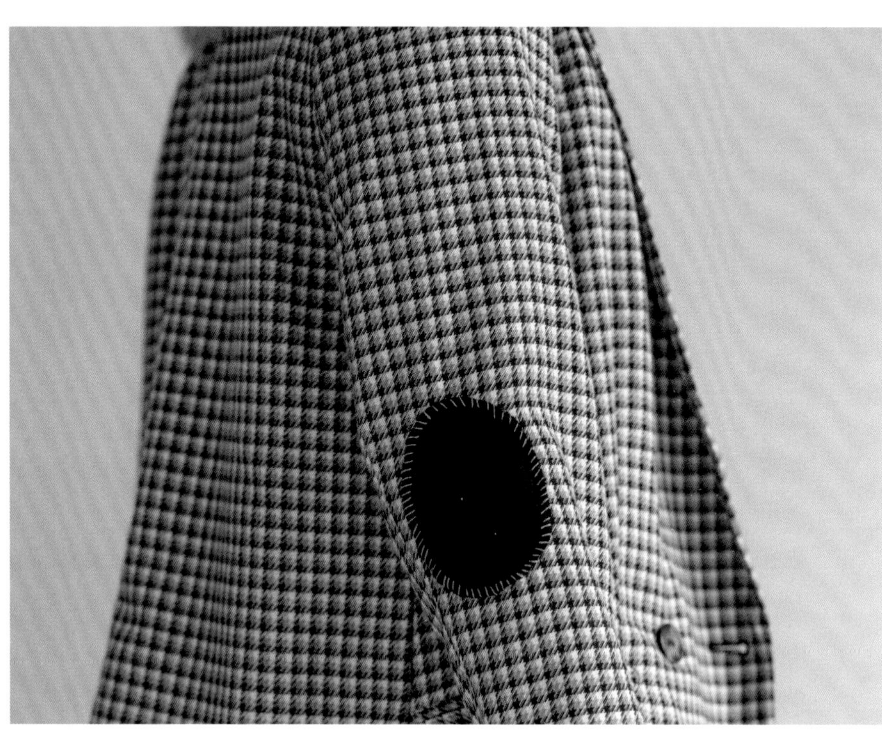

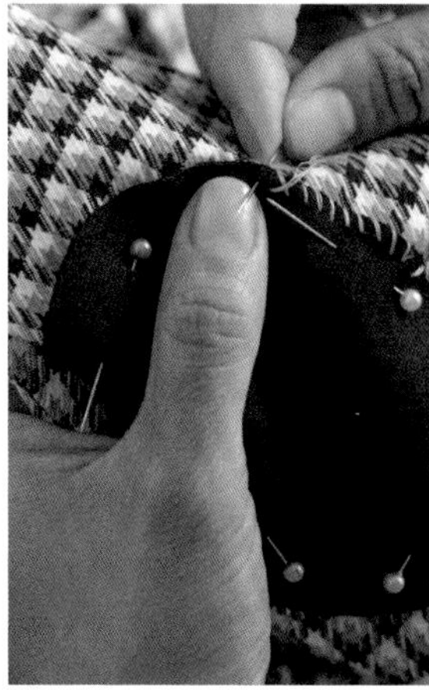

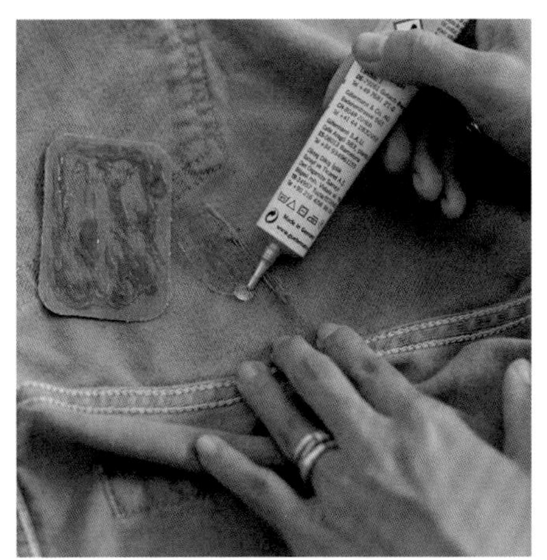

Patching a pair of jeans

There are several ways to patch a pair of jeans and we would like to highlight two methods. The first is a quick fix for those who want to save time and the other is for those who want to try a more advanced and creative technique.

PATCH WITH FABRIC GLUE

If you're pressed for time, fabric glue offers an alternative to sewing. Fabric glue, sometimes called fabric adhesive, is ideal for patching rips and holes in thicker fabrics. It should saturate the textile fibers without soaking all the way through. Keep in mind that this may not be a permanent solution. The patch will stay on for a few washes but not forever.

You'll need:
Denim patch
Fabric glue

STEP 1: Cut a piece of denim fabric that fits over the hole. Apply fabric glue to the back and inside edges of the patch, covering the margin around the tear in your jeans.

STEP 2: Attach the patch over the hole from the inside of the jeans. To make sure the fabric glue sets properly, place a heavy object on top of the patch until the glue dries. Just be careful not to accidentally glue together another layer of fabric in the process.

Advanced patching with sashiko

If you really want to get creative, you can use sashiko, the Japanese embroidery technique mentioned earlier. Sashiko is a form of visible mending where the point is to purposely add a new aesthetic to your garment rather than restoring its original look.

You'll need:
Patch
Cotton thread
Needle

STEP 1: Place the patch on the inside or outside of the hole, depending on the look you want, and pin it in place.

STEP 2: Thread a needle and tie a knot at the end of the thread. Sew small running stitches back and forth across the surface until they form a symmetric pattern. The stitches should be the same length or slightly longer than the spaces between them.

STEP 3: Attach the thread with a few stitches.

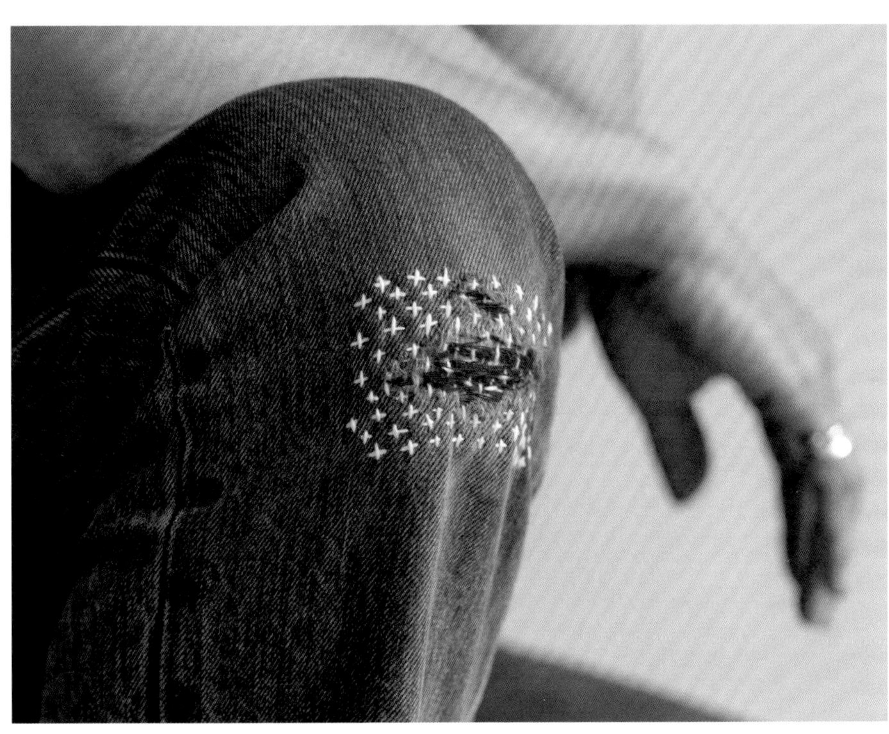

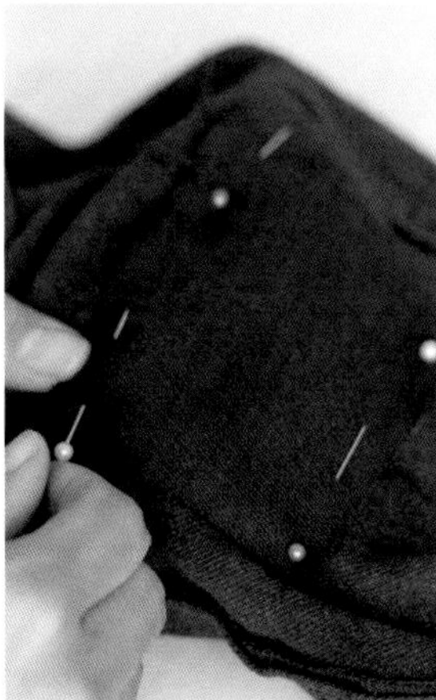

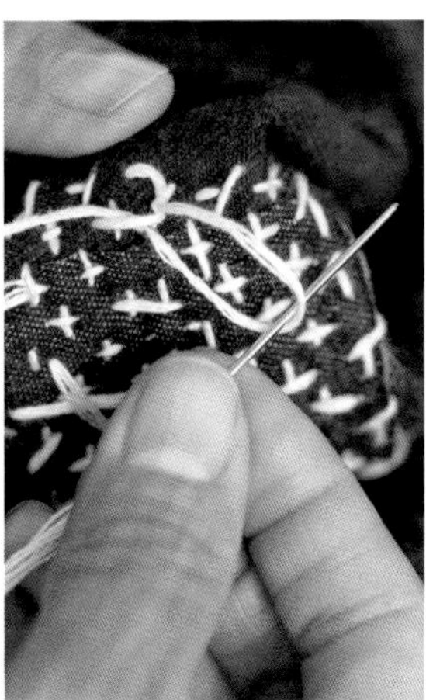

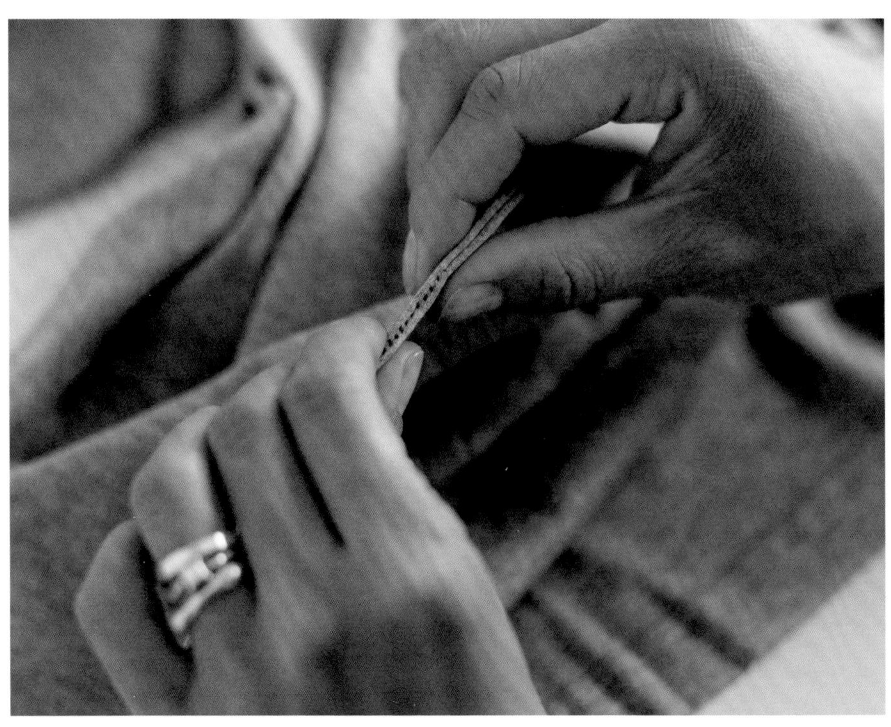

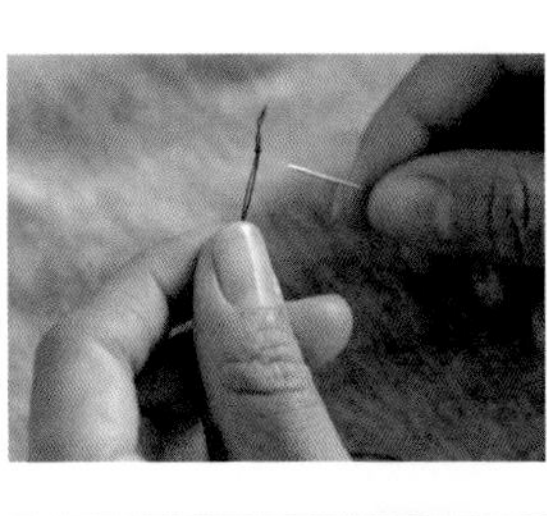

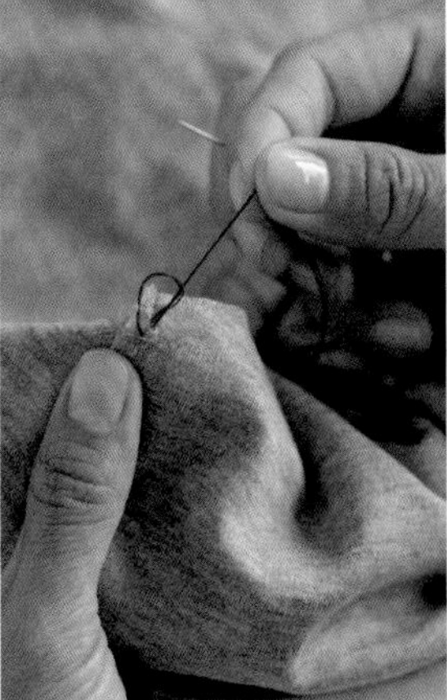

Hems

A hem is a method of finishing off a garment, where the edge of a piece of cloth is folded and sewn to prevent the fabric from unraveling and to adjust the length. However, it is not unusual for a hem to break. Most people have probably found that threads sometimes start to hang at the bottom of a shirt or a pair of trousers. When that happens, the hem has loosened. In this section we go through how to mend a loose hem.

SEW A HIDDEN HEM

A hidden hem is a hem that you can't see, placed on the inside of a garment. It is most common on garments like a dress, a skirt or a pair of pants.

You'll need:
Thread
Needle
Scissors

STEP 1: Thread a needle, tie a knot at the end of the thread and turn the garment inside out.

STEP 2: Cut loose threads from the broken hem.

STEP 3: Start stitching a bit into the old seam by using ladder stitches. To make the stitch less visible, insert the needle in as few threads as possible on the face side of the fabric. Continue sewing a bit into the old seam.

STEP 4: Attach the thread with a few stitches.

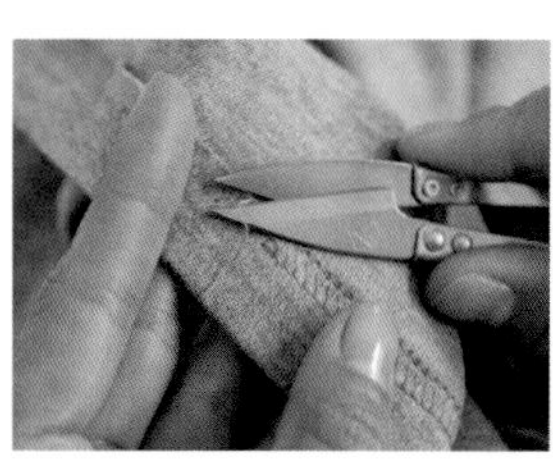
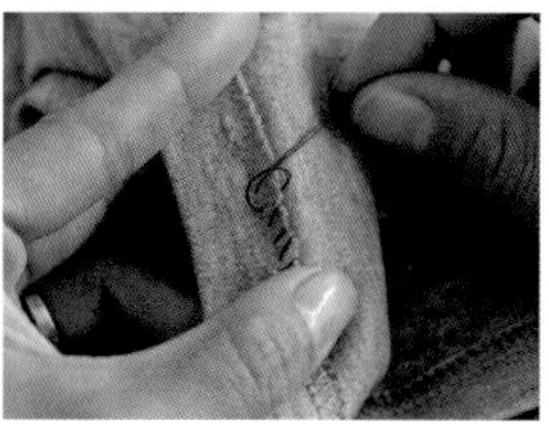
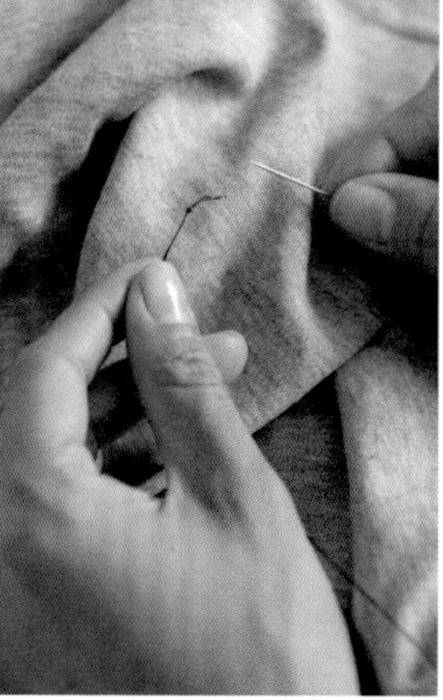
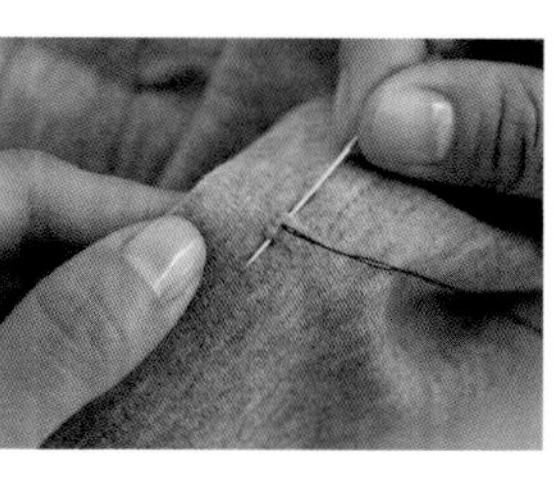
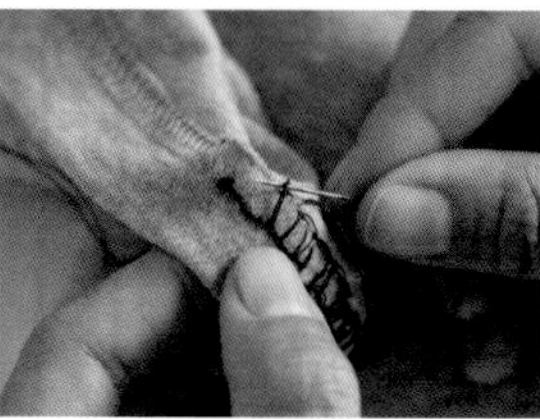

Mend a visible hem on a T-shirt or shirt

A visible hem is the opposite to a hidden hem. It is a hem that you can see on the outside of garments, most commonly on T-shirts.

You'll need:
Thread
Needle
Scissors

STEP 1: Turn the garment inside out. Cut the loose threads and pull them into the hem using a needle.

STEP 2: Thread a needle and tie a knot at the end of the thread.

STEP 3: Sew whip stitches to the same width as the existing seam.

STEP 4: Turn the fabric inside out. Place the needle in the penultimate stitch. From the fabric's face side, place another needle, to make sure the new hem follows the existing hem. Continue sewing in the same stitch length as the original hem. Do not tighten, as the fabric will wrinkle.

STEP 5: Attach the thread with a few stitches.

Zippers

Zippers can easily get stuck but also come loose from the fabric if you pull too much. In this section we go through some tricks on how to fix a broken or slow zipper.

MEND A BROKEN ZIPPER

It is not uncommon for a zipper to loosen from the fabric of a shirt or a dress. With a few simple mending tips, you can quickly sew the zipper back into place.

You'll need:
Thread
Needle
Scissors

STEP 1: Thread a needle and tie a knot at the end of the thread. Turn the garment inside out. Position the zipper so that you can see where it's broken.

STEP 2: Attach with needles to hold the fabric in place. Cut loose threads.

STEP 3: Sew a stitch a bit into the old seam. Sew the next stitch, starting in the middle of the previous one. Repeat until you have sewn across the entire hole.

STEP 4: Attach with a few extra stitches.

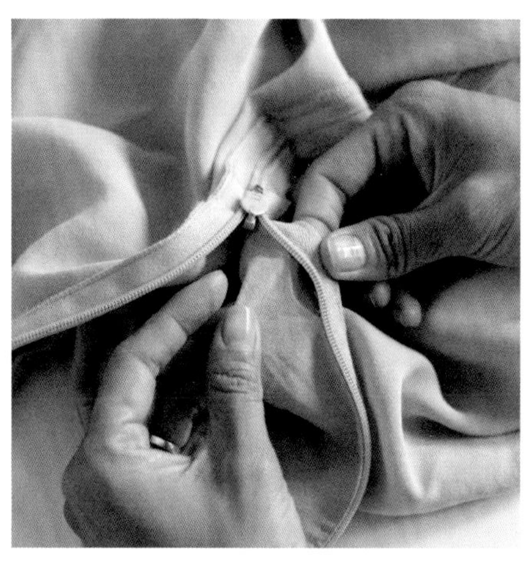
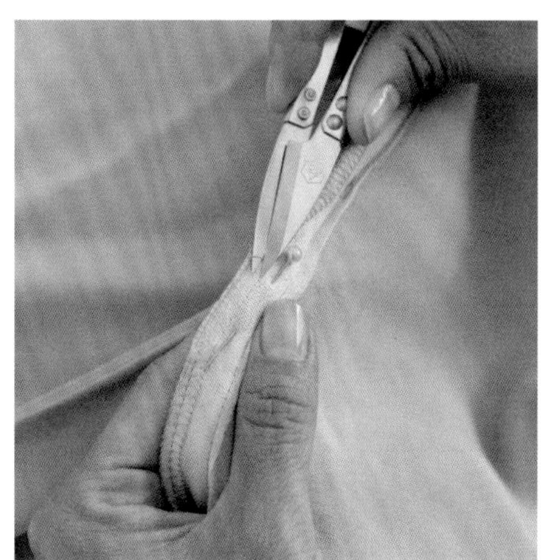
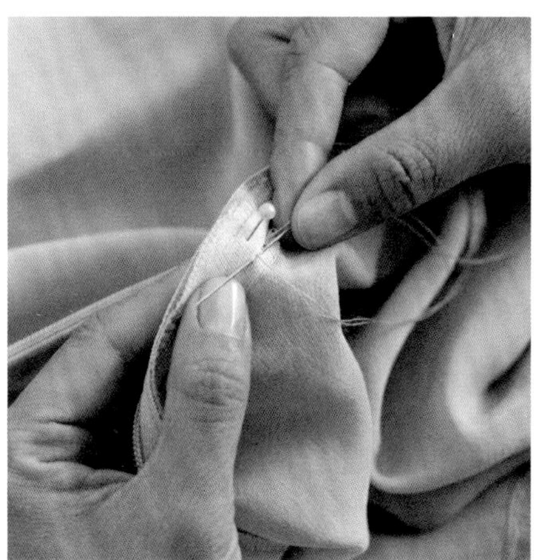
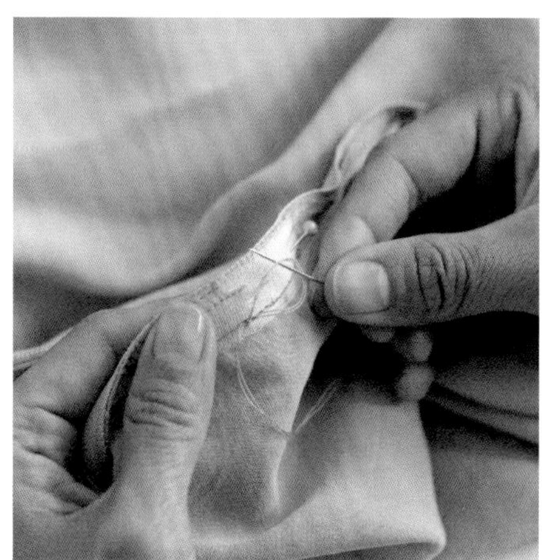

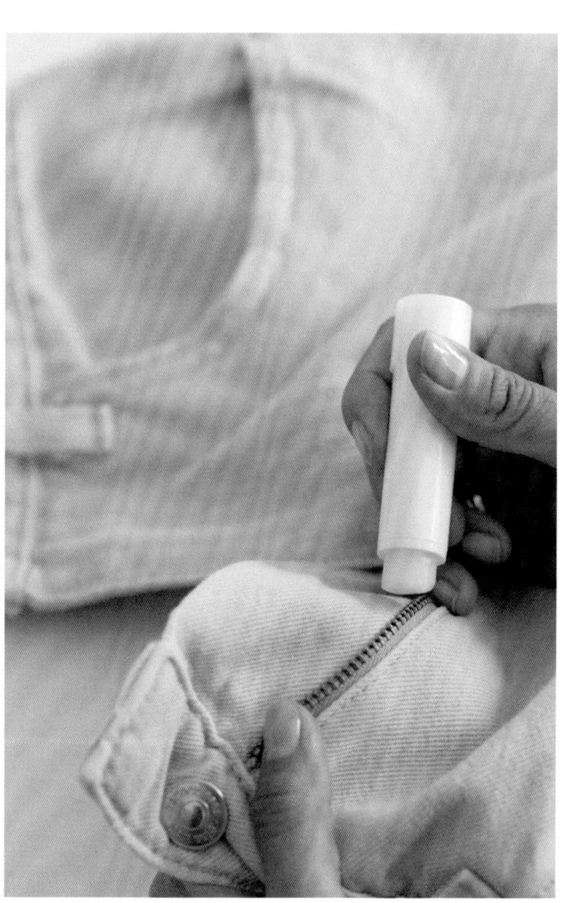

HOW TO FIX A SLOW ZIPPER

If you have a zipper that is moving slowly or getting stuck, there are a few things you can try.

LUBRICATE THE ZIPPER: You can lubricate the zipper by applying a small amount of wax or soap to the teeth of the zipper. This will help the zipper slide more smoothly.

CHECK FOR DEBRIS: Sometimes dirt, lint or fabric fibers can get caught in the zipper, causing it to move slowly or get stuck. Use an old toothbrush to gently clean the teeth of the zipper.

CHECK FOR BENT TEETH: If the zipper teeth are bent or misaligned, this can cause the zipper to move slowly or get stuck. Use a pair of pliers to gently straighten any bent teeth.

CHECK FOR A BROKEN SLIDER: If the zipper slider is broken or damaged, this can also cause the zipper to move slowly or get stuck. You may need to replace the slider with a new one.

CHECK THE FABRIC: Sometimes, the fabric of the garment can get caught in the zipper, causing it to move slowly or get stuck. Gently pull the fabric away from the zipper teeth as you zip up or down.

Buttons

Almost everyone has experienced a button falling off a shirt, dress or pair of trousers at some point. As frustrating as it may be, it's one of the easiest repairs that any beginner can do with the right tools.

SEWING A BUTTON ON A SHIRT

You'll need:
Thread
Needle
Scissors
Button

STEP 1: Remove old threads and place the button in the right place. Thread a needle and tie a knot at the end of the thread. Start from the back and place the needle in one of the holes.

STEP 2: Leave a few millimeters between the button and the fabric. Sew three stitches straight across or on the diagonal. Place the needle in the next hole and repeat.

STEP 3: Spin three to five times around the threads under the button to create a 'neck' for the button. Attach by sewing through the 'neck' a few times.

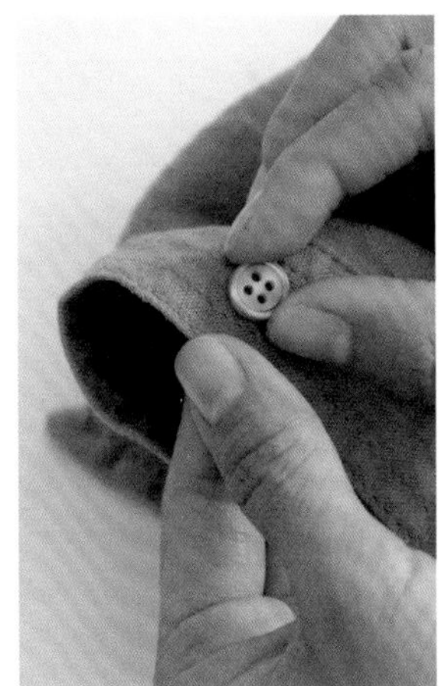

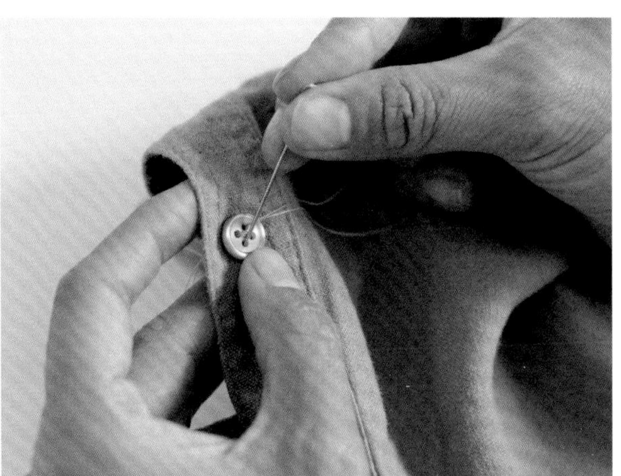

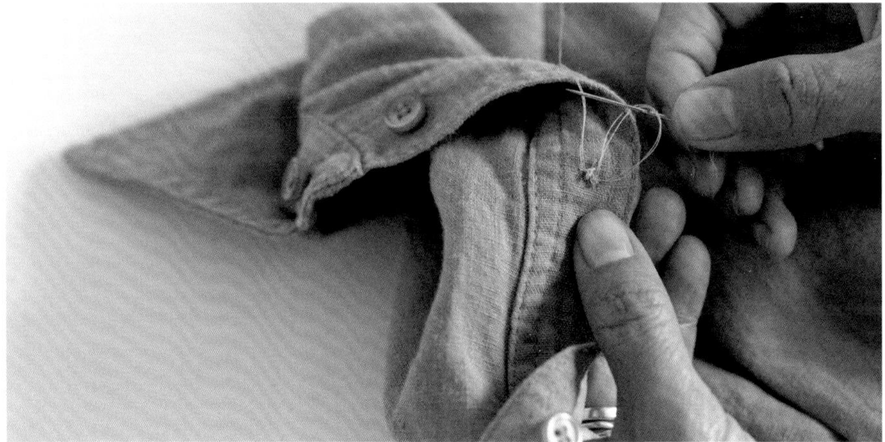

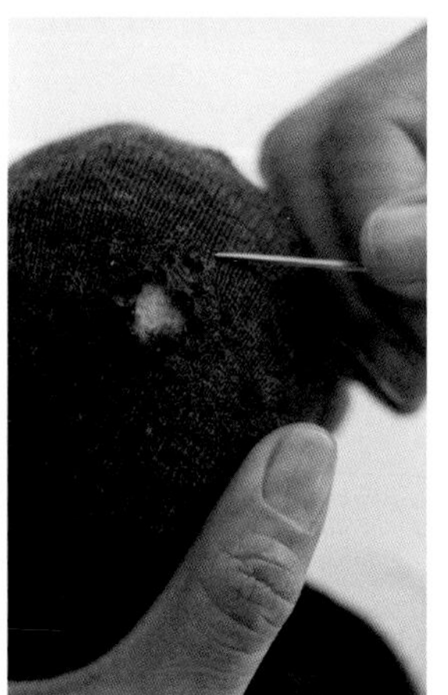

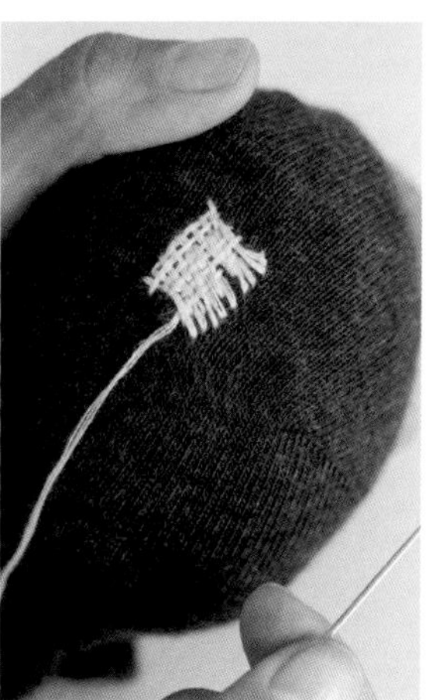

Repair a sock

Having a hole in the heel doesn't mean the sock has reached the end of its life. The best way to repair smaller holes is to use the darning technique with a thicker thread and long perpendicular stitches that are woven together over and around the hole.

You will need:
Darning needle
Thread in a matching color and material to the sock
Scissors
Darning egg (or a small ball or lemon)

STEP 1: Turn the sock inside out and stretch the damaged area over a darning egg, a small ball or a lemon, making it easier to see and work on. Thread the needle and tie a knot at the end of the thread.

STEP 2: Begin darning by weaving the needle over and under the threads of the intact fabric, perpendicular to the direction of the knit. This creates a sturdy base for the rest of the repair. Once you have created a solid base, start weaving the thread back and forth in a parallel direction to the original knitting, covering the hole as much as possible.

STEP 3: Continue weaving the thread back and forth over and under the new threads until the hole is completely covered, and the repair is level with the rest of the sock. Make sure the stitches are tight and close together to create a strong repair. When you have finished darning, tie off the thread on the inside of the sock with a knot.

Make do

Making do with what you have is just as important as mending. All textiles, no matter how torn they are, can become something new. It's all about being creative and finding fresh ways to find inspiration in what you already own.

Upcycling and downcycling

Regardless of how worn a piece of clothing is, you can always find new ways to use it. This is what upcycling and downcycling are all about, minimizing textile waste and finding new uses for clothes. But what is the difference between the two?

Upcycling means that you increase the value of an item by sewing a different item out of it. You can, for example:

- Turn an old T-shirt or jeans into a tote bag.
- Use the fabric from old jeans to create a patchwork quilt or a denim jacket.
- Turn an old sweater into a pillow cover or a pair of mittens.
- Use the fabric from an old shirt to make a new apron.

Downcycling means that you find a new use for the item that has less value than the original item. You can, for example:

- Turn old T-shirts into cleaning rags.
- Use old textiles as crafts for your children.
- Use old sweaters for insulation.

All of these examples are great ways to repurpose sweaters and reduce textile waste.

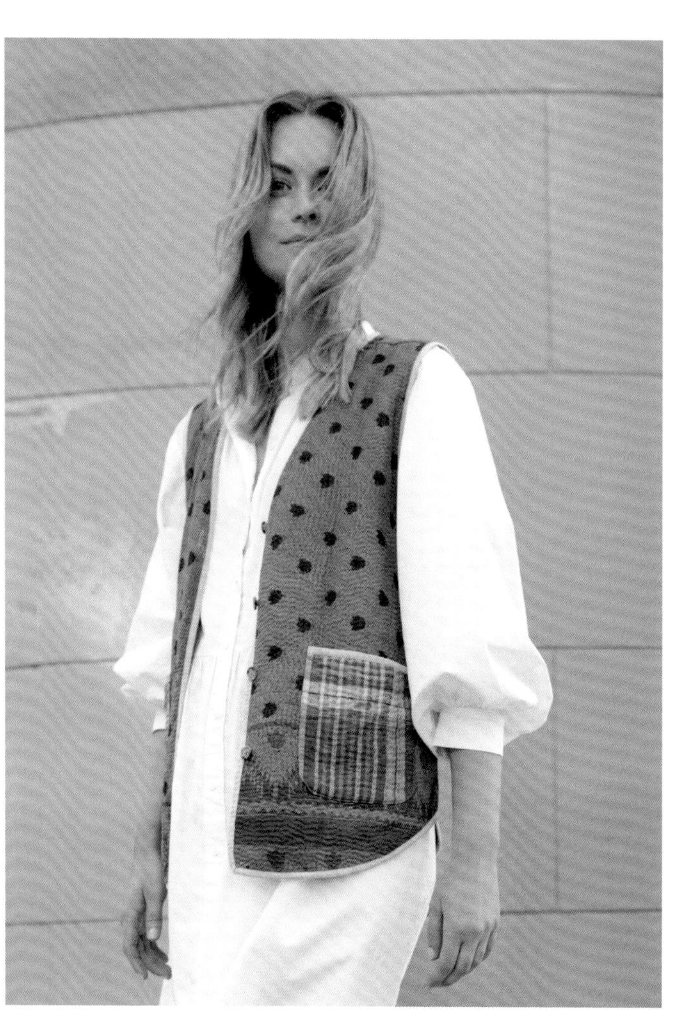

Remake or redesign

There are several ways to renew the clothes you already own by remaking or redesigning. Dare to challenge yourself and find new ways to update your wardrobe.

A good idea is to start with garments that don't hold any sentimental value for you, so you experiment and find your way. Here is a list of great remakes to try out and get inspired by:

CUT IT

The easiest way to remake a garment is to cut the fabric. Start by cutting ripped jeans into shorts or removing sleeves from a sweater to create a T-shirt. Remember to use fabric scissors as this makes the process much easier and will give you a better result.

EMBROIDERY

This is a decorative technique that involves sewing different designs onto fabric using thread, yarn, or other materials. It can be used to add patterns, images or text. Embroidery is great for updating your wardrobe in a fun, creative and easy way.

COLOR BLENDING

Dyeing garments is a great way to update clothes that may have lost their luster. There are different ways to dye clothes; textile paint is one of them. It is super easy, and you will find all the instructions you need on the bottle. But if you don't like to use chemicals, you can try making natural color using food. Examples of foods that work are red wine, tea, onions, red cabbage, coffee, turmeric and avocado.

TRANSFORMATION

Upcycling old textiles into new garments can give you a completely new wardrobe. Be creative and play with it. Transform an old dress into a skirt or a top, turn an old scarf into a handbag or a belt or create a dress from old curtains. With a little bit of creativity, there are endless possibilities.

How to color clothes with food

STEP 1: Add water to a large saucepan along with your selected food and boil for about 30 minutes.

STEP 2: Carefully remove the food from the saucepan [using a slotted spoon].

STEP 3: Add the garment and reheat but do not boil. Leave for at least an hour, reheat as needed if water cools.

CREATE PATTERNS WITH STEAM

You will need:
Steamer
Color pigments
Pot
Colander
Foil
Rubber band

STEP 1: Wet the garment with water. Choose colors and spread as desired over the garment. Roll up from any direction. Wrap it in foil and tie with a rubber band.

STEP 2: Place the garment in a colander over a pan of steaming water. Let the garment steam for two hours.

STEP 3: Wash, dry and steam with a steamer.

Dye it

TIE-DYEING

Tie-dyeing is believed to have originated in several cultures, including ancient China, India, and parts of Africa and South America.

In tie-dyeing, sections of the fabric are folded, twisted or tied with string or rubber bands before applying dye. The tied areas resist the dye, creating distinctive patterns and color variations when the fabric is submerged in dye. The patterns produced by tie-dyeing are typically characterized by bold, psychedelic and random designs with vibrant colors. The final result is often a kaleidoscope of colors and abstract shapes.

BATIK

Batik is a traditional wax-resist dyeing technique that originated in Indonesia. It has a long history in Indonesian and Javanese culture and has been used for centuries to create intricate designs on fabric.

In batik, hot wax is applied to specific areas of the fabric using a tool called a tjanting or a brush. The wax acts as a resist and prevents the dye from penetrating those areas. After the wax is applied, the fabric is submerged in dye, and the process can be repeated with different colors to create intricate, detailed patterns.

Once the dyeing is complete, the wax is removed to reveal the final design. It has a diverse range of applications and creates more graphic patterns. It has been used for traditional clothing like sarongs and shirts, as well as for decorative items, wall hangings and artistic pieces.

SHIBORI

Shibori is a traditional Japanese resist-dyeing technique that dates back to the eighth century. It has a rich history in Japanese culture and was used to create various patterns on kimono fabric and other textiles.

Shibori involves folding, twisting or binding fabric before dyeing it. The fabric is often secured with string, rubber bands or wooden pegs, creating patterns when the fabric is dyed. Shibori typically creates more subtle, organic patterns.

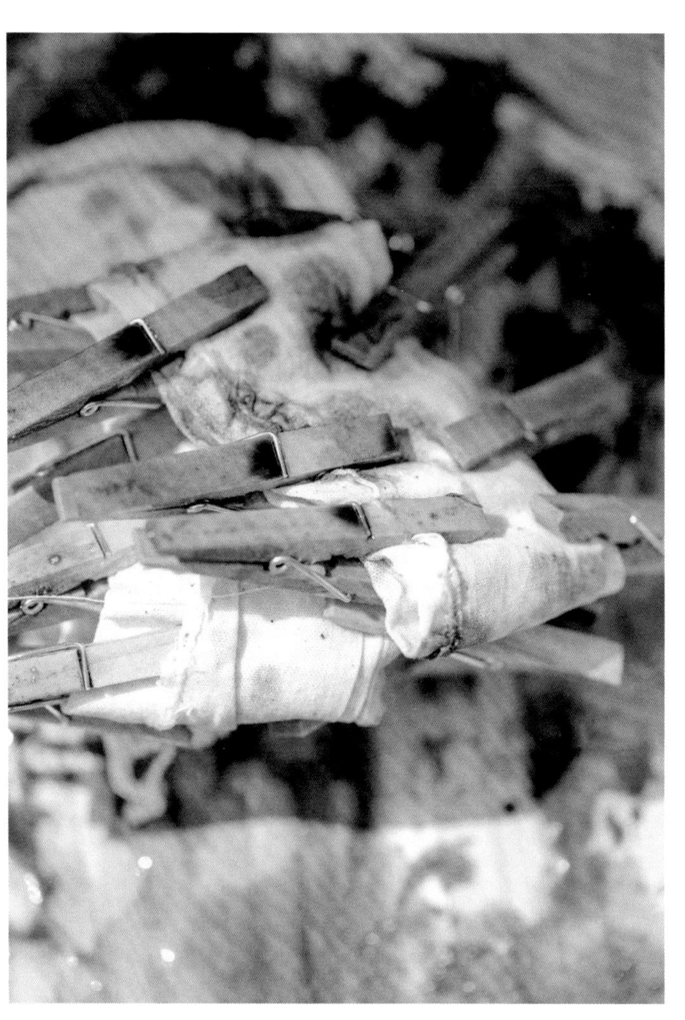

CHAPTER 4

THE FUTURE OF CLOTHING CARE

We all need to slow down. Given the state of the fashion industry today, it can sometimes feel like 'conscious fashion' is an oxymoron; that the very idea of using clothing to express your style is intrinsically tied to materialism, excess and overconsumption. But here we want to challenge you to envision a brighter future – a Steamery utopia where clothing and conscious choices can be reconciled in a more harmonious way.

The truth is we need to change our behaviors and learn to make do with less. This includes learning to share items with others rather than owning them, being conscious about what we choose to buy, as well as learning to make things last for as long as possible. In this chapter, we will share our vision for the future and what needs to happen to make this vision come to life, but also explore some emerging trends and predictions about the future of the fashion industry, textile production and clothing care.

In our Steamery utopia, we can embrace what has already been produced. We should swap and care for all the beautiful clothes that exist, and we can recycle and reuse textiles that have reached the end of their first life cycle.

A slow philosophy

We hope that people learn to find value in the soothing and meditative aspects of clothing care. Instead of relying on retail therapy and buying new clothes to calm our stressed minds, we can find comfort in caring for what we already own. Whether that is steaming a piece of clothing and slowly watching the fabric come back to life, reviving a cashmere sweater by trimming off its pilled surface with a fabric shaver or taking the time to hand wash your most treasured garments, these routines can become a moment of true tranquility. Essentially, we should learn to treat these clothing care routines like enjoyable spa moments for our clothes, rather than tedious chores.

As Steamery's mission is to help you keep your clothes looking beautiful, we are constantly looking to improve and simplify traditional clothing care tools as well as inventing new ways to make clothing care easy, effective, and more appealing in the future. Up until now our research and development includes smoothing out wrinkles, enhancing textures and colors, maintaining and improving fit, minimizing tear, refreshing and washing, tackling stains and graying, removing pilling and reviving your clothes' surface as well as mending and alteration. Our goal is to provide the tools and knowledge so you can restore a damaged garment to its original quality and feel fulfilled in the process.

However, in our clothing care utopia, we also appreciate small signs of wear on garments, like patina, giving unique character and charm, reflecting a unique story and the history they hold.

Our vision for the future

SHARING WARDROBES

The very idea of owning items of clothing should be old news. Our philosophy is that you never really own a garment; you are only caring for it before handing it over to the next owner. In the future, we foresee a rise in rental and swap services where consumers can share wardrobes and rotate garments on a regular basis. Readily available and flexible services will allow people to rent, borrow, repair and maybe even learn how to make their own clothes in communal, collaborative settings. Freedom of expression and the visual intrigue of fashion will live on without the need for excessive shopping and mass-produced clothing.

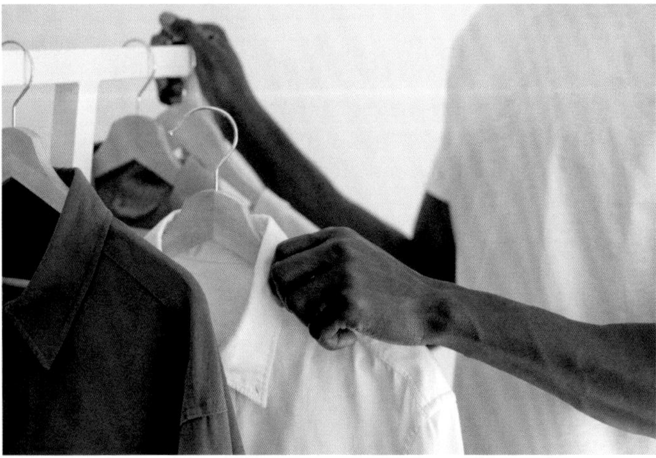

CLOTHES LIBRARIES

In addition to rental and swapping services, we could also imagine free public lending libraries for clothes becoming a popular trend. The idea is not too far out of reach. People already lease and rent cars and we borrow books with a library card even though they are also sold new at a full price.

The concept of a clothes library is especially applicable to garments that we typically only wear once or twice in a lifetime, like a wedding dress or an extravagant gown for a one-off event. Again, this does not have to replace the idea of clothes ownership, but it can certainly complement it. Imagine owning a limited capsule wardrobe of reliable clothes for everyday wear, but seeking out a rental service or clothes library when you feel the need to get more dressed up. Seems entirely doable, right?

A REPAIR REVOLUTION

One key piece of the puzzle is to make it easier for the everyday person to mend and repair clothes. Going to a tailor to alter clothes feels like an old-fashioned habit for most ordinary consumers, especially those on a tight budget. But the mend-and-repair industry could evolve into a more accessible service and make it easier to order repair services from the convenience of your home. Providing a flexible service where you get your clothes repaired in a smooth way, an at-your-door pickup service and delivery of the repaired garment.

Mending and repairing can also be incredibly relaxing and meditative activities to enjoy with friends and family. In our vision for the future, mending and sewing clubs could be as common as book clubs and clothes-swap gatherings. It could become a mindful habit that helps people wind down and do something productive together.

QUALITY OVER QUANTITY

It will become more important for fashion consumers to appreciate the benefits of choosing quality over quantity. Better-quality garments don't just feel a lot nicer to wear but should also last a lot longer than items that were made more cheaply. And if you have a wardrobe that is made up of fewer, higher-quality items that you truly love, you'll be more invested in taking care of them and making sure they last. Remember though, that a higher price point doesn't always mean a garment is better quality. A basic knowledge of textiles and clothing care will help you to distinguish the garments that are truly made to last for a long time.

INCREASED TRANSPARENCY

In the future, we hope that every piece of clothing will come with a clear and comprehensive care label that details the production and supply chain of the garment before it ends up on the sales floor.

With increased transparency, customers can feel empowered to make fully informed decisions on whether a garment is right for them. By knowing more about what makes up the clothes they own, consumers will understand how to take care of their garments so that they last a lifetime.

LOCAL MARKETS AND SMALL-SCALE PRODUCTION

We are beginning to see the development of ultra-local marketplaces and small-scale production. More and more, people are supporting locally grown and produced goods - you can see this particularly with breweries and coffee roasters. People want to support and give back to their local communities. Concepts such as farm-to-table dining can apply to fashion as well. It can serve the purpose of reducing the distance from producer to consumer, which makes it easier to understand how long it takes to sew a garment.

As consumers grow more aware of the unethical nature of fast fashion, the market can move further away from large-scale fashion, replacing it with small business owners, local artisans and initiatives that support slow fashion.

MO-6716S

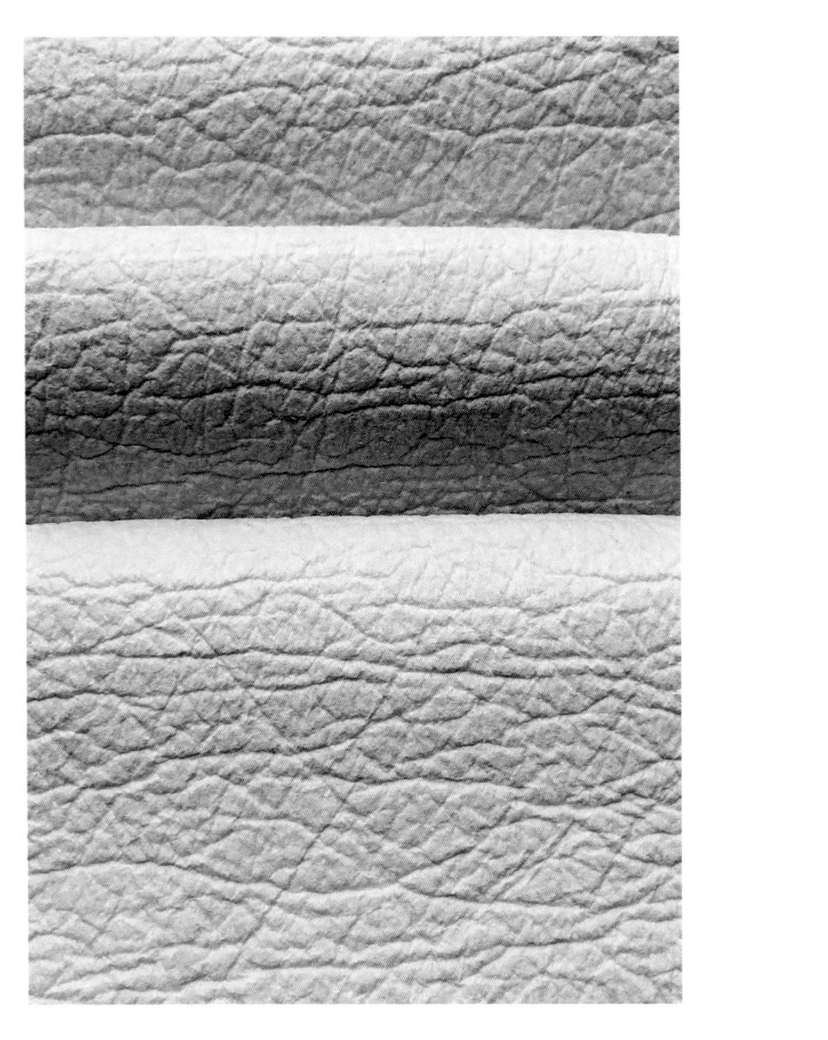

Innovations in the textile industry

Pioneering textile engineers are innovating their craft like never before. We are making new fabrics from materials that would have been unthinkable a few years ago. Here are a few emerging trends and new discoveries that look set to revolutionize the textile industry:

UPCYCLING WASTE

Some designers are producing bio-textiles from agricultural and food industry waste, helping to use up resources that would otherwise harm our environment. Famously, ocean waste is being upcycled into new materials such as Econyl®, which is made from recycled nylon yarn from fishing nets, textile production scraps and other synthetic waste. Sneakers are also being made with recycled ocean plastic.

CLEVER LEATHER

There is now a wide range of plant-based leathers that are being used by designers. Some, such as wine leather and apple leather, use leftover fruit skin to make their products, while pineapple leather utilizes the leaves stripped from the fruit when it's harvested. Rather than using leftover resources, mushroom leather uses mycelium – a network of fungi grown on beds of organic matter in a vertical farming facility.

BREAKTHROUGHS IN TEXTILE RECYCLING

While up until now it's been quite difficult to recycle most fabrics, it is becoming increasingly possible to repurpose fiber blends and divert textile waste from landfills.

Mistra Future Fashion, a research program based in Sweden, has been doing just that. In 2017 they revealed Blend Re:wind, a process that makes it possible to separate and recycle mixed-textile clothing such as cotton-polyester blends. The reclaimed fibers can then be used as new raw materials in existing textile manufacturing processes. While it will take time for these recycling practices to be implemented throughout the world, it is an important milestone towards the future of the global textile recycling systems necessary to enable circularity in the fashion industry.

Recycled Polyester (or rPET) is a step foward and made when used plastics are either melted down and made into a piece of material, or chemicals are used to revert the polyester back to new plastic. While it's still being developed, the idea is one step closer toward achieving a closed loop system, where materials can be continuously used with minimal waste. Similarly, scientists are also working on creating recycled nylon from car tires. Like many plastics, it's very difficult to recycle tires, so the continued development of effective recycling techniques would make a huge difference to the plastic we use that goes to waste.

Digitizing the shopping experience

Remember the iconic opening scene of the '90s movie *Clueless*, where the main character Cher is seen choosing her outfit from a database of her own closet, testing out different combinations on a digital image of herself? This scene may not be a far stretch from how we will choose and try on garments in the future. Modern technology is already starting to revolutionize the way we shop and interact with fashion, and brands will have to adjust how they create and sell clothing to make it work in a digital world as it continues to evolve.

ARTIFICIAL INTELLIGENCE

It could soon be possible to try on a garment before it is even made. Artificial intelligence (AI) and augmented reality (AR) technology can help create immersive and accessible virtual try-on experiences that allow consumers to visualize how garments will look and fit their bodies without physically trying them on. This technology will enable shoppers to help create their dream garments digitally, which can save hundreds of hours of physically manufacturing these pieces. By involving consumers at the start of the design process, brands can test demand for a product before physically launching it on the market, thus reducing the number of unsold clothes.

VIRTUAL FASHION

In some cases, you may not even have to buy physical garments anymore. With the invention of digital avatars and filters, fashion brands have been designing and launching virtual collections. Although this will never replace the need for physical clothes, it can serve as a means to express your style without contributing to textile waste.

In Meta's metaverse, users can purchase full looks from Puma and Prada to dress their personalized avatars. Meanwhile, digital supermodels are booking gigs with high-end fashion brands and modeling real designs on their social media accounts. These AI-generated influencers are blurring the lines of fiction and reality and sparking conversations about the possibility of tech displacing real humans working in the fashion industry.

The first ever AI Fashion Week debuted in April 2023 in New York City. The show featured runway scenes created with a variety of imaging software. It was a way for up-and-coming virtual fashion designers to gain exposure and three winners, selected by popular vote, were given the opportunity to create their own designs to be sold as physical garments. In the future virtual fashion will likely continue to evolve and find a way to coexist with the traditional fashion industry.

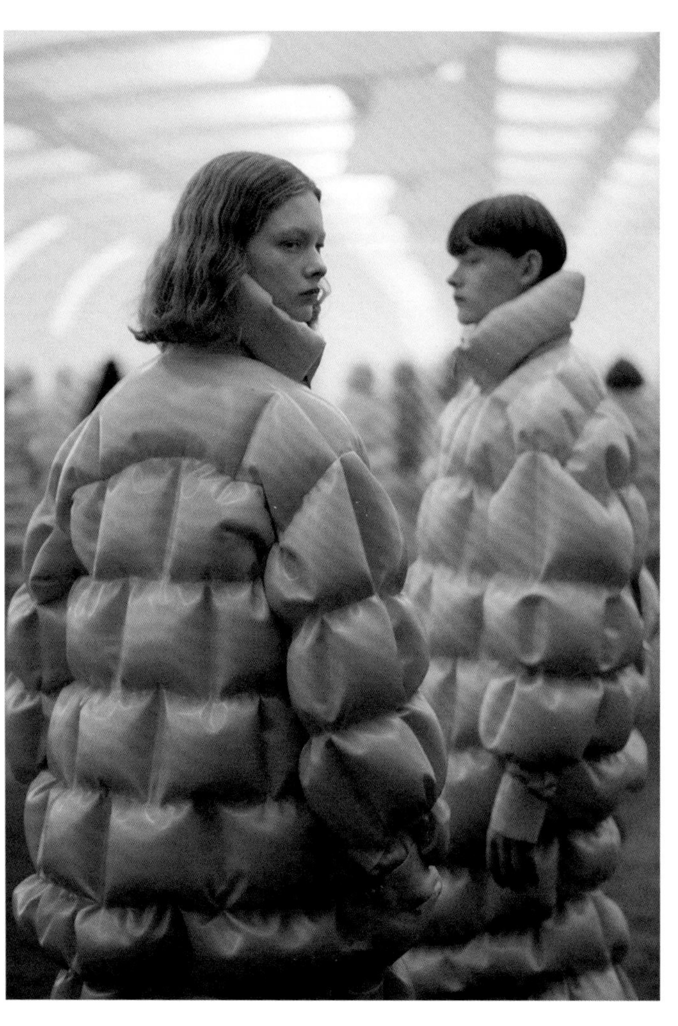

3D PRINTED FASHION

With the help of 3D printing technology, fashion can become more accessible and customizable than ever before. As 3D printers become more common to have and own, clothing and accessories can be printed out on demand.

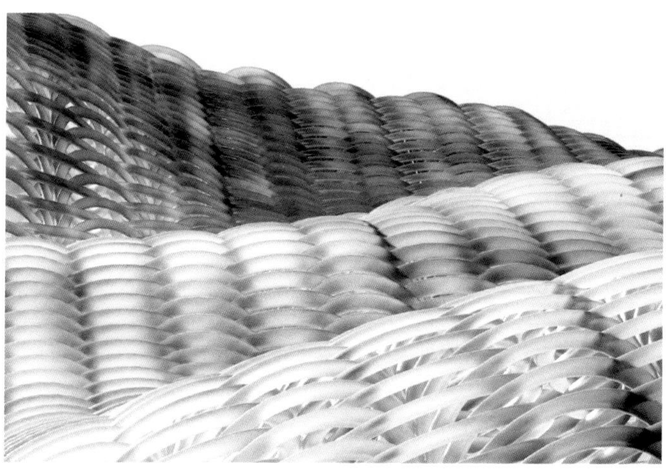

What can you do as a consumer?

Solving the problems in the fashion industry can feel overwhelming, but we can start on a small scale and create a ripple effect by challenging ourselves to change our habits for the better and practicing good clothing care. For example, think about supporting the brands that are using these new technologies in order to encourage wider changes to the way we produce and consume clothes.

If you're unsure where to start, why not take inspiration from our nine challenges? You can use some or all of these challenges to set yourself goals to work toward being a conscious consumer and a clothing care expert.

CHALLENGE 1: WEAR YOUR CLOTHES WITH PRIDE

It's time to say goodbye to feeling pressured to show up in new clothes to work every day. As we grow more conscious about the environmental footprints of our closets, constantly buying new clothes won't work in the long run. Wearing your favorite garments again and again is something to strive for and is the new way to live.

This shift has already happened in other aspects of life. People started carrying around reusable steel water bottles to drink from in order not to buy new plastic bottles, and fabric totes replaced plastic bags. This same idea can be applied to the world of fashion, by making a habit of wearing the same garment a couple of days in a row.

CHALLENGE 2: THINK ABOUT BUYING LESS

While some people like to challenge themselves to the extreme by not shopping for an entire year, it's simply a good idea to consider buying fewer clothes. This challenge is a very personal one so we would encourage you to set your own parameters based on what you think is doable. Remember, it'll feel a lot better to achieve a manageable goal than not achieve one that is more difficult. Then, if you've completed one challenge, you can try pushing yourself further the next time.

Once you've set your parameters, write them down and try and stick to them. It's also a good idea to write a checklist on your phone to look at if you find that you're close to making a purchase that is not necessary. Think about if you really need the item or if you'd be devastated if they didn't have the piece in your size.

CHALLENGE 3: BECOME A MENDER

Invest in a basic sewing kit and keep it in a place where you can easily access it. Challenge yourself to repair and remake something in your wardrobe, like patching an old pair of jeans or turning an old T-shirt into a tote bag. Having a patched-up hole in your jeans is a visual statement that communicates that you are resourceful and that you care about making your clothes last, limiting textile waste. It also adds character to your style in a way that new, mass-produced fashion never could.

If the mending tips in Chapter 3 felt too far out of reach, it could be a good idea to take a sewing class to get started. There are plenty of sewing classes available online too. If mending isn't your thing, why not start supporting your local tailor?

CHALLENGE 4: ORGANIZE A CLOTHES SWAP

Challenge yourself to organize clothing events like a clothes swap with friends or at work. It's actually very simple. All you have to do is set a date, ask your colleagues or friends to go through their wardrobes and clear out items they know they don't use anymore and want to pass on to the next owner. Then you collect all the clothes and organize them properly on clothes racks. Everyone who participates can take home whatever clothes they want from the racks to have in their closets. In this way, you will all get new clothes without buying anything new. To keep things a little more organized, set a maximum limit of five items per person so everyone gets something they really appreciate and like.

CHALLENGE 5: FOLLOW FEWER TRENDS

It is about time to stop following trends like our lives depend on it. The new trend is all about creating a capsule wardrobe with timeless items that you can mix and match with each other. Invest in clothes that you know you will use for years to come and learn how to take care of them, so they last. That way, you can rotate your wardrobe and find inspiration over and over again in the clothes you already own. Ask yourself if you really want that dress that everyone else owns. Personal style is an expression of you, how you are, and what you stand for. Be proud of your own personal style and don't be afraid to wear your favorite pieces day after day.

CHALLENGE 6: OPT FOR SECOND-HAND

One of the most important changes we need to make when it comes to the clothing industry is to opt for second-hand first. Producing a garment requires significant amounts of chemicals, water, energy and other natural resources. And even if changes are being made to improve the industry and the materials produced, an item produced can never be better than if it hadn't been made in the first place. Let's face it, there are enough clothes on this planet already.

CHALLENGE 7: THINK TWICE BEFORE WASHING

Remember to wash your clothes only when necessary. There are plenty of great alternatives you can try to extend the time between washes. Steam, remove stains, air out overnight and mist your clothes regularly. Also give hand washing a go. Washing less will extend the life of your wardrobe and also save a lot of energy and water. And when you do need to wash, always wash full loads and use the right detergent. When in doubt, read the care label to know exactly how to treat and wash different kinds of materials. You could even see what happens if you only steam your garments - chances are it'll keep your clothes looking great. Remember steam is used in lots of products beside steamers. Why not try a steam program on your washing machine if it has one?

CHALLENGE 8: AVOID THE TUMBLE DRYER

Challenge yourself to avoid the tumble dryer as much as you can. Tumble drying is bad from many perspectives but, most of all, the heat and movement can shrink, tear and misshape your clothes. We do not recommend that you tumble dry anything but bed linen and towels.

CHALLENGE 9: SUPPORT LOCAL SLOW FASHION INITIATIVES

Our final challenge is to support and purchase locally grown and produced goods. Keep an eye out for small business owners, local artisans and initiatives in your community that support slow fashion. We need to go back to how things were before when clothes were tailored and custom-made. If we know more about the process and who made the clothes we wear, it is easier to show respect to the craftsmanship and preserve the clothes in good condition. And if you get an item tailored to make it fit you perfectly, chances are you'll care more about keeping that garment looking amazing.

Remember that it's okay to take things at your own pace. The first and most important step is to start thinking about your wardrobe in a conscious way. You don't have to adopt all these new habits this week, and this is certainly not a battle to fight on your own. We can all play a part in shaping the future of fashion that we want to see.

‘Join us in this journey of mindful clothing care, where we celebrate the beauty of well-loved clothes and cherish the memories they hold. Together, let’s make a positive impact for ourselves and the planet by extending the life of our beloved garments and most importantly finding joy in the process.’

Frej Lewenhaupt

References

p.12

Remy, N. Speelman, E. and Swartz, S. (2016) Style that's sustainable: A new fast-fashion formula. McKinsey. https://www.mckinsey.com/capabilities/sustainability/our-insights/style-thats-sustainable-a-new-fast-fashion-formula.

United States Environmental Protection Agency. (2018) Facts and Figures about Materials, Waste and Recycling. https://www.epa.gov/facts-and-figures-about-materials-waste-and-recycling/textiles-material-specific-data

p.22

Bravo, L. (2020) How to break up with fast fashion, p. 105-106. Headline Home.

p.47

A.K. Chapagain A.Y. Hoekstra H.H.G. Savenije R. Gautam. (2005) The water footprint of cotton consumption. Unesco-IHE. Institute for water education. https://waterfootprint.org/resources/Report18.pdf

p.77

United States Environmental Protection Agency. (2018) Facts and Figures about Materials, Waste and Recycling.

p.78

Bravo, L. (2020) p. 209-211.

p.80

Fulop, L. (2020) Wear, repair, repurpose, p. 15-19. The country man press.

p.183

Dahlén, J. & Leymann, J. p. 137.

p.207

Johansson, J. & Nilsson, J. (2016) Slow Fashion - din guide till smart och hållbart mode, p. 150–173. Ordfront.

p.213

Dahlén, J. & Leymann, J. (2022) Klä barnen - växa, ärva, fixa laga, p. 162-167. Ordfront.

p.232

De La Motte, H. and Palme, A. (2020) The development of the Blend Re:wind process. https://www.ri.se/sites/default/files/2020-02/The%20development%20of%20Blend%20Rewind_0.pdf

p.234

Maslavi, S. (2023) The Future Of Fashion: Exploring How Artificial Intelligence Is Transforming The Market. Forbes, 10 February. https://www.forbes.com/sites/forbesbusinesscouncil/2023/02/10/the-future-of-fashion-exploring-how-artificial-intelligence-is-transforming-the-market/

p.235

Yotka, S. (2022) Balenciaga, Prada, and Thom Browne will dress your meta avatar. Vogue, 17 June. https://www.vogue.com/article/balenciaga-prada-thom-browne-meta-instagram-avatar.

Ruberg, S. (2023) Virtual AI supermodels trigger wider fears in fashion workforce. NBC News, 30 April. https://www.nbcnews.com/business/business-news/ai-models-levis-controversy-backlash-rcna77280.

p.237

Van Herpen, I. (2020) Iris van Herpen Imagines a Fashion Future in Which Clothes Are Only Made on Demand. Vogue, 19 May. https://www.vogue.com/article/fashions-front-lines-iris-van-herpen.-

Washing symbols

Wash at max. 30°C (85°F)

Wash at max. 40°C (105°F)

Wash at max. 60°C (140°F)

Gentle wash cycle

Not machine washable

Drying symbols

Tumble drying allowed

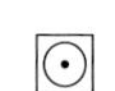
Tumble dry on gentle program

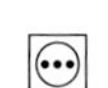
Tumble dry on high program

No tumble drying

Hang dry

Drip dry

Flat dry

Dry cleaning symbols

Dry clean only

Do not dry clean

Ironing symbols

Iron at max. 110°C (230°F)

Iron at max. 150°C (300°F)

Iron at max. 200°C (395°F)

Do not iron

Do not steam

Bleaching symbols

Bleaching allowed

Non-chlorine bleachable

Not bleachable

Index

Photography credits

IMAGES

Camilla Svensk
6, 10, 14, 20, 34, 37, 38, 40, 50, 53, 54, 56, 62, 64, 84, 86, 95, 96, 100, 101, 105, 109, 110, 115, 118, 121, 124, 137, 147, 148, 152, 155, 158, 161, 168, 179, 181, 185, 188, 191, 192, 195, 196, 198, 201, 202, 205, 206, 211, 224, 238, 244, 246

Photographers Hugo Ljungkvist and Karl Wirenfelt
130, 140

Photographer Osman Tahir
122

Pexels.com
13, 18, 46, 49, 79, 132, 177, 217, 222, 229

Photographer Sophia Schyman
69, 72

Unsplash.com
76

Wikicommons
230

Photographer Sarah Medina Lind
28, 33, 83

AI creator José Sobral – "airsuits by paatiff"
236

Designer Oskar Håkansson
237

Photographer Vincent Fillon for FabBRICK
233

COVER AND ILLUSTRATIONS

Cherro Yanjie Wang

Acknowledgements

A journey would be nothing without the people you meet along the way, the ones with whom you share and develop ideas, and the ones you choose to join forces with. Creating this book would not have been possible without the expertise of our panel: Adrian Zethraeus, Jennie Dahlén, Anne-Charlotte Hanning, Sofia Westin and Jonas Hofgren. Their contributions and knowledge of the fashion industry, mending, textiles and clothing production have been invaluable.

I would also like to thank the whole Steamery team, particularly the internal project group working on this book: Lisa Segersson, Karolina Hall, Rebecca Rendahl and Lisa Wirenfelt. You have all demonstrated, yet again, that anything is possible with passion and dedication. And, of course, a huge thank you to Penguin Random House for collaborating with Steamery to publish this book and share our mission with the world. Step by step, we are getting closer to bringing out the full potential of our wardrobes.

I would also like to extend my thanks to everyone who has worked with Steamery from the beginning to where we are today. I am forever grateful to all the team members who have contributed to Steamery's success. The start-up years of Steamery were the most exciting journey I have ever witnessed and it is a result of the energy bringing together dedicated individuals with passion for clothing care. I would also like to thank all our suppliers, sales partners and resellers who have welcomed Steamery into their businesses. Most importantly, I am grateful to our customers who have embraced clothing care and shared their routines with others, inspiring more people to join the slow fashion movement.

Lastly, I would like to express my deepest gratitude to my co-founders, Martin Lingner and Petra Ringström, for planting the seed of Steamery and making it grow. I am also grateful to our Art Director, Cherro Yanjie Wang, who joined us at an early stage and played a significant role in developing our brand and concept.

I truly hope that reading this book helps you feel inspired to learn more about our philosophy of clothing care and incorporate some of this knowledge in your everyday life.

- Frej Lewenhaupt, Co-founder & CEO at Steamery

1

Published in 2024 by Ebury Press, an imprint of Ebury Publishing
20 Vauxhall Bridge Road, London SW1V 2SA

Ebury Press is part of the Penguin Random House group of companies
whose address can be found at global.penguinrandomhouse.com

Design: Clare Sivell
Production: Percie Bridgwater
Publishing Director: Elizabeth Bond
Project Editor: Fionn Hargreaves

This edition first published in Great Britain in 2024
www.penguin.co.uk

A CIP catalogue record for this book
is available from the British Library

ISBN 9781529918953

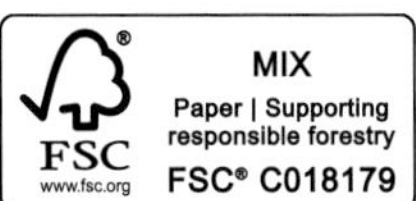

Penguin Random House is committed to a sustainable future for
our business, our readers and our planet. This book is made
from Forest Stewardship Council® certified paper.